Brooker + Stone

form+
structure

The organisation of interior space

n. the visible shape or
configuration of something

n. the arrangement of
and relations between the parts or
elements of something complex

An AVA Book

Published by AVA Publishing SA
Rue des Fontenailles 16
Case Postale
1000 Lausanne 6
Switzerland

Tel: +41 786 005 109
Email: enquiries@avabooks.ch

Distributed by Thames & Hudson (ex-North America)
181a High Holborn
London WC1V 7QX
United Kingdom

Tel: +44 20 7845 5000
Fax: +44 20 7845 5055
Email: sales@thameshudson.co.uk
www.thamesandhudson.com

Distributed in the USA & Canada by:
Watson-Guptill Publications
770 Broadway
New York, New York 10003
USA

Fax: +1 646 654 5487
Email: info@watsonguptill.com
www.watsonguptill.com

English Language Support Office
AVA Publishing (UK) Ltd.

Tel: +44 1903 204 455
Email: enquiries@avabooks.co.uk

ISBN 2-940373-40-X and 978-2-940373-40-6

10 9 8 7 6 5 4 3 2 1

Design by John F McGill
Cover image by Emma Cross, courtesy of Multiplicity

Production by AVA Book Production Pte. Ltd.,
Singapore

Tel: +65 6334 8173
Fax: +65 6259 9830
Email: production@avabooks.com.sg

Form + structure

Name:
D.E. Shaw Office and Trading
Area, reception

Location:

Contents

Form + structure

Contents

The aim of this book is to provide a focussed, informative and readable investigation into the practice of designing interior space. Interior architecture is a subject that encompasses the analysis and understanding of existing buildings and proposed spaces, the nature and qualities of an interior space, and an intimate examination of the characteristics of interior decoration. Form & Structure will reveal the process of organising and redesigning a particular space or spaces and will dismantle this practice into its constituent parts with a particular emphasis upon issues of form and structure. Each section will focus on the space but will also deal with a particular aspect of the redesigning process. It will argue that the way forward for interior design is a method based upon process rather than function. An approach based upon a perceptive and discriminating reading of the existing or proposed space can produce both dynamic and appropriate results.

Name:
ING & NNH offices
Location:
Budapest, Hungary
Date:
1997
Designer:
Erick van Egeraat (EEA)

Form + structure

Section headers
Each chapter is broken down into sub-sections, the title of which can be found at the top left-hand corner of each spread.

Section introduction
Each sub-section is introduced by a short paragraph, outlining the content to be covered.

Page numbers
Page numbers are displayed in the top right-hand corner of each spread.

Definitions & descriptions

014+**015**

Interior architecture, interior design and interior decoration are all practices that deal, in varying degrees, with an existing space or building. This section will outline the nuances between the different disciplines.

Interior architecture

Name:
Tate Modern

Location:
London, UK

Date:
2000

Designer:
Herzog & de Meuron

Interior architecture is concerned only with the remodelling of existing buildings; that is the development of attitudes towards existing spaces and structures, building reuse and organisational principles. It bridges the practices of interior design and architecture, often dealing with complex structural, environmental and servicing problems. This practice encompasses a huge range of project types, from museums, galleries and other public buildings, through office and other commercial buildings to domestic developments.

When remodelling the enormous Bankside Power Station for use as an art gallery, the approach Herzog & de Meuron took was to accentuate the particularly huge and industrial qualities of the building. The gallery spaces occupy the appropriate rooms around the edge of the building, while the vast turbine hall has become an internal public street. The most dramatic and obvious element of the remodelling is the insertion of a massive lantern, or glazed roof, which hovers along the central axis of the building. It functions as a lightwell during the day, throwing natural light into the public space at the centre of the gallery, and at night it appears to glow with the latent energy of the obsolete power station. Although the function of the building has completely changed, the inherent qualities of it have not: the same massive, strong and powerful characteristics of the power station have been transferred to the gallery.

Top:
The interior of the Tate Modern
The new lightweight glazed lantern hovers above the sheer bulk of the existing building.

Above:
Turbine Hall
The entrance sequence.

Above:
The exhibition hall
Natural light flows through the axial lantern of the turbine hall.

Left:
Axonometric drawing of the building
The massive public space in the turbine hall is apparent in this cut away drawing.

Introduction > **Definitions & descriptions** > Reuse & redesign

The design process

Chapter footers
The current chapter is displayed in the bottom left-hand corner of each spread.

Section footers
Past, present and future sub-sections are listed in the bottom right-hand corner of each spread. The current sub-section is highlighted in bold.

Form + structure

Important information
Each case study is introduced by name, location, date and designer.

Captions
All captions carry a directional and title for easy reference.

Assemble: Focus study 2

Name:
Fendi Showroom

Location:
Paris, France

Date:
2002

Designer:
Lazzarini Pickering Studio

Lazzarini Pickering devised a geometric language for the flagship Fendi showroom in Paris. The concept, which characterises the opulent luxurious brand, is internationally transferable. The image is opulent, dynamic and generous; long sculptural elements of architectural proportions interact three-dimensionally with each other. The units climb towards the centre climb to form a three-dimensional sculptural staircase, emphasising the upper floors, while others slide delicately through the shop, exaggerating the length and space, thus ensuring that the entire shop is on view. The units that touch the edges of the space, (that is the floors and the walls) are of dark wood, those in the middle of raw waxed steel. The orthogonal order of these display fittings allows the clothes to be placed informally, almost carelessly, encouraging the customers to linger and touch. Rearranging the seasonal exhibits is a simple and straightforward task in the minimal interior.

The collection of simple basic forms, of strong dark elements against plain white painted walls creates a dramatic interior of light and shade.

'…like our furniture, the all-important thing about our architecture is that it must be transformable. That's why we need a departure point. A point that contains centrifugal forces, an idea around which the whole project can pivot.'

Claudio Lazzarini

Above:
View through the space
The dynamic quality of the furniture creates an illusion of three-dimensional movement.

Facing page, above:
Interior display elements
Accessories are placed almost carelessly upon the sliding planes.

Facing page, below:
Three-dimensional drawing of the interior
Display units organise and accentuate the volume of the interior.

Transferability
The concept for a particular assembled interior can be transferred to anywhere in the world, because there is little relationship between the building and the new interior, it is really only a matter of how much of the design can be used at each location.

Autonomous interiors

Disguised + **Assembled** + Combined

Pull quotes
Additional quotes from subject experts and practitioners are displayed in light grey, slanting boxes at the top of pages.

Diagrams
Where possible, diagrams are used to illustrate the technical aspects of each project.

Boxed texts
Additional points of interest to the reader are displayed in grey boxes.

How to get the most out of this book

Unlike many other design- and art-based disciplines, which often begin with the theoretical stance of the artist, the design of an interior is always influenced by the experience of the place that it is to inhabit. The practice of designing interiors is an intricate process of satisfying the needs of the users, while balancing this with considerations of situation and place. This opening chapter will introduce the notion of interior architecture, interior design and the strategic reuse of buildings. It will examine the fundamental ideas that underpin the design of interior space, and will also clarify the different approaches to conservation: from the preservation of the building in its found condition to the comprehensive redevelopment of the whole structure.

Name:
Groninger Museum

Location:
Brugge, the Netherlands

Remodelled:
2003

Designer:
514NE

Definitions & descriptions

Interior architecture, interior design and building reuse are all disciplines that deal with the development and design of interior space. The interior architect or designer will transform a given space, whether the crumbling ruins of an ancient building or the drawn parameters of a building proposal. This complex process requires an understanding of the qualities of the given existing building, while simultaneously combining these factors with the functional requirements of new users. Before looking in more detail at how the interior architect or designer does this, it is essential that the various interpretations of the subject are carefully analysed and understood.

Interior design is a term that has traditionally been used to describe all types of interior projects. This would have included everything from decoration to remodelling. However, in view of the fact that building reuse has become such a highly regarded practice, it has clearly become necessary to divide the main subject and define more clearly the individual specialisms: interior architecture and design, processes that deal with the manipulation of the three-dimensional volume must not be confused with interior decoration, which generally concentrates on furniture and finishes.

Above:
Castelvecchio Museum, Verona.

Reuse & redesign

The reuse of existing buildings and the redesign of spaces within them are subjects that are central to the evolution of the urban environment, and issues of conservation and sustainability have become vital to the development of cities. As the manner in which the urban environment has changed, so the prevailing attitude towards building reuse has also altered.

There are a number of different methods used in the conservation of a structure and there are distinct differences between each approach: preservation maintains the building in the found state; restoration is the process of returning the condition of the building to its original state; renovation is the practice of renewing and updating a building and remodelling, or adaptation, is the process of wholeheartedly altering a building. Sometimes two of the methods may be employed in unison, for example, when designing the Sackler Galleries at the Royal Academy of Arts in London, Foster Associates ensured that the façades of the original buildings were completely restored before embarking on the remodelling of the space.

It is important that the designer is aware of the requirements of the new users of the building or space. Without an understanding of these, it is not easy to establish the exact qualities of design required and it is difficult to appreciate whether a relationship with the original building can be established.

Above:
Sackler Galleries, Royal Academy of Arts.

Interior architecture, interior design and interior decoration are all practices that deal, in varying degrees, with an existing space or building. This section will outline the nuances between the different disciplines.

Interior architecture

Name:
Tate Modern

Location:
London, UK

Date:
2000

Designer:
Herzog & de Meuron

Interior architecture is concerned only with the remodelling of existing buildings; that is the development of attitudes towards existing spaces and structures, building reuse and organisational principles. It bridges the practices of interior design and architecture, often dealing with complex structural, environmental and servicing problems. This practice encompasses a huge range of project types, from museums, galleries and other public buildings, through office and other commercial buildings to domestic developments.

When remodelling the enormous Bankside Power Station for use as an art gallery, the approach Herzog & de Meuron took was to accentuate the particularly huge and industrial qualities of the building. The gallery spaces occupy the appropriate rooms around the edge of the building, while the vast turbine hall has become an internal public street. The most dramatic and obvious element of the remodelling is the insertion of a massive lantern, or glazed roof, which hovers along the central axis of the building. It functions as a lightwell during the day, throwing natural light into the public space at the centre of the gallery, and at night it appears to glow with the latent energy of the obsolete power station. Although the function of the building has completely changed, the inherent qualities of it have not: the same massive, strong and powerful characteristics of the power station have been transferred to the gallery.

Top:
The interior of the Tate Modern
The new lightweight glazed lantern hovers above the sheer bulk of the existing building.

Above:
Turbine Hall
The entrance sequence.

Above:
The exhibition hall
Natural light flows through the
axial lantern of the turbine hall.

Left:
**Axonometric drawing
of the building**
The massive public space
in the turbine hall is apparent
in this cut away drawing.

Above:
Long view of the interior
The basement terrace is
animated through occupation.

Interior design

Name:
Children's Galleries,
Science Museum

Location:
London, UK

Date:
1995

Designer:
Ben Kelly Design

Interior design is an
interdisciplinary practice
concerned with the creation
of a range of interior environments
that articulate identity and
atmosphere through the
manipulation of spatial volume,
placement of specific elements,
such as furniture and the
treatment of surfaces. It generally
describes projects that require
little or no structural changes
to the existing building, although
there are many exceptions to this.
The original space is very much
retained in its original structural
state and the new interior is
inserted within it. It often has
an ephemeral quality and typically
would encompass such projects
as retail, exhibition, domestic
and office interiors.

In their design of the Children's
Galleries at the Science Museum,
Ben Kelly Design has developed
a distinct approach to interior
design that is based upon the
manipulation and reuse of found
objects, combined with an
explicit sense of structure and
a desire to expose the truth about
a particular situation or space.
The practice became known for
the 'industrial chic' look that was
developed in the 1980s for the
infamous Haçienda club and
Dry 201 bar in Manchester.
The Children's Galleries at the
Science Museum adopt that
same attitude: the space has
been stripped down to leave only
the essential elements; that is,
the raw walls, floors and ceiling.
The ducts, cables and other
services are revealed – even the
cladding around the lift has been
removed so that workings are
exposed. The space has then
been animated with 'industrial'
objects and motifs to create
an open place where children
can feel sufficiently relaxed
to enjoy themselves, yet suitably
stimulated to become curious.

'Interior design had come to the forefront of public design-consciousness through its leadership of the retail revolution…'

Anne Massey

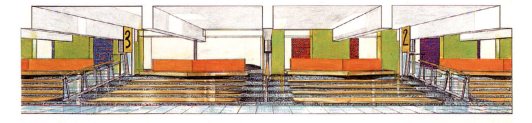

Above:
Drawing of the terrace
Three-dimensional drawing showing the formal collection of carefully placed objects.

Left:
The terrace
The rhythm of the existing building dictates the position of the distinct spaces within the new interior.

Left, below:
The old and new combined Ben Kelly uses a palette of industrial materials.

'Rooms may be decorated in two ways: by superficial application of ornament totally independent of structure, or by means of those architectural features which are part of the organism of the house, inside as well as out.'

Edith Wharton & Ogden Codman Jr

Interior decoration

Name:
St Peter's Cathedral

Location:
Lancaster, UK

Date:
1995

Designer:
Francis Roberts Architects

Interior decoration is the art of decorating interior spaces or rooms to impart a particular character that fits well with the existing architecture. Interior decoration is concerned with such issues as surface pattern, ornament, furniture, soft furnishings, lighting and materials. It generally deals only with minor structural changes to the existing building. Typical examples of this practice are the design of domestic, hotel and restaurant interiors.

A very fine example of professional decoration is the project for St Peter's Cathedral, Lancaster. The Victorian cathedral was reordered in the 1970s and many of its artefacts were taken away. Francis Roberts Architects completely restored the building in 1995; they redecorated it in a gothic revival style and designed new furniture and artefacts. The decoration on the walls and ceiling is appropriate to the style of architecture. The exposed beams and other structures are intricately painted and gilded; the ceiling and walls are more simply decorated with stencilled motifs. The new furniture includes a carved stone altar, brass corona and iron sanctuary gates.

This project was completed in September 1995 and received a RIBA award in 1996. A review of the project was published in *Church Building*, January 1996: '…here is an architect who understands the fin de siècle architectural mind not only in an extremely thorough, but also practical way. He can actually create buildings in that design-language; the rest of us can only talk about it.'

Above:
Sketch of the interior
The qualities of space and light are revealed in this drawing.

Facing page:
The cathedral
The heavily decorated chancel contains the new brass corona, the iron sanctuary gates and the carved stone altar.

Introduction > Definitions & descriptions > Reuse & redesign

This section will discuss the various approaches
to the creation of interior space within buildings.
It will outline practices from preservation, right the way
through to the creative adaptation of existing structures.

Above:
Dun Troddan wall
The broch is delicately
constructed from varying sizes
of dry stone.

Preservation

Name:
Dun Telve and
Dun Troddan Brochs

Location:
Glenelg, Scotland

Date:
About 2,000 years ago

Preservation is a practice that
maintains the building or structure
in its found state, however ruinous
that may be. The building is
made safe and any further decay
is prevented from occurring; the
ruined condition is important
to the historical understanding
of the place.

An extraordinary example of
preserved structures is the series
of brochs built about 2,000 years
ago in the north of Scotland.
Brochs are tall stone towers,
up to about eight metres high.
Built from two concentric circles
of dry stone, they were both
defensive and protective. The
gap between the walls provided
sufficient space for living,
sleeping and circulation, possibly
with different wooden floor levels
within the structure, while the
ground level centre area was
probably used for the animals.
The building was most likely to
have had a timber roof.

These structures have been
preserved in their ruinous state,
the possibility of any further
decay has been prevented, but
no attempt to return them to their
original condition has been made.

Above:
Dun Troddan Broch
The concentric circular structure
is clearly visible amongst the ruin.

**Society for the Protection
of Ancient Buildings**
William Morris founded the Society
for the Protection of Ancient Buildings
(SPAB) in 1877. The society's aims
are to preserve and repair buildings, with
respect to their age and character. They
regard the romance and authenticity
of the building as important and advise
on the methods and skills necessary
to retain this.

Definitions & descriptions > Reuse & redesign

Restoration

Name:
Villa Savoye

Location:
Poissy, France

Date:
1929

Designer:
Le Corbusier

Restoration is the process of returning the condition of the building to its original state, and this often involves using materials and techniques of the original period to ensure that the building appears as it would have when constructed. This type of approach is typically used to conserve precious or listed buildings such as churches and other historic buildings, where the method of occupying them has not drastically changed. One of the most obvious problems with this approach is that historic buildings have often been added to, changed or substantially altered during their history and so there is a question as to which of these states the building should be restored to.

Another important consideration is the reason for the restoration: For what purpose is the building to be restored? Is it so that it can remain within the collective memory as a reminder of where we have come from? Or will that leave it useless and unfit for any modern use?

A typical example of this type of project is Le Corbusier's modernist masterpiece, Villa Savoye. It was originally constructed in 1929 as a weekend country home, but it now stands as a monument to the five points of architecture: free façade, free plan, pilotis or columns, active roof space and horizontal windows. It is now little more than a museum of architectural promenade.

Above:
The villa in the landscape
Post-restoration.

Facing page:
Villa Savoye in ruins
The building before restoration.

The International Charter for the Conservation and Restoration of Monuments and Sites

The International Charter for the Conservation and Restoration of Monuments and Sites (The Venice Charter, 1964) is a document that gives an international framework for the preservation and restoration of ancient buildings. The intention of the charter is to safeguard these sites as both works of art and as historical evidence.

'Most of the work on older buildings affects their interiors. Not only must designers or architects be competent with current code requirements, structural realities, mechanical and electrical services, and economic restrictions, but they must be knowledgeable of architectural and social history.'

John Kurtich & Garrett Eakin

Renovation

Name:
The Rookery

Location:
Chicago, USA

Date:
1992

Designer:
Thomas 'Gunny' Harboe

Renovation is the process of renewing and updating a building. The function will remain the same and the structure is generally untouched, but the manner in which the building is used will be brought up to date. It is usually the services that require attention, especially the heating and sanitary systems. A good example of refurbishment is a large mansion that will be adapted for twenty-first-century living but not substantially changed.

The renovation of the court lobby of the Rookery was a complex process of balancing the conservation of the original 1888 building with several previous renovations of the building and the needs of the present users. The narrative of the journey through the eleven-storey cast-iron frame masonry and terracotta office block by original architects, Burnham & Root, had been compromised by the progressive alterations, as had the natural light through the glass roof and the vertical circulation. The 1905 renovation by Frank Lloyd Wright continued the spatial journey through the building and clad the cast-iron columns with white marble. Thomas Harboe was anxious to embrace this work, while erasing the subsequent alterations, so a datum of 1910 was set. The original circulation route was re-established, the entrance vestibule was restored to Wright's design and Burnham & Root's original marble mosaic floor was rebuilt. Most importantly, a new glazed roof was built above the original, which eliminated any problems of water ingress and reinstated the former brilliantly lit courtyard. This whole process adapted the building for twenty-first-century expectations and use.

Right:
View through the main foyer
The Rookery prior to restoration.

Below:
The light-filled space
The renovation makes the priory
once again fit for purpose.

Above:
Threshold
The route processes through the old city wall.

Facing page:
The Cangrande statue
The statue is placed at the pivotal point within the building.

Remodelling

Name:
Castelvecchio Museum

Location:
Verona, Italy

Date:
1957–1964

Designer:
Carlo Scarpa

Remodelling is the process of wholeheartedly altering a building. The function is the most obvious change, but other alterations may be made to the building itself, such as the circulation route, the orientation, the relationships between spaces. Additions or extensions may be constructed, while other areas may be demolished. This process is sometimes referred to as adaptive reuse, especially in the USA, or as reworking, adaptation, interior architecture or even interior design.

Carlo Scarpa was essentially, the forerunner of an approach based upon a sympathetic understanding of the existing building and he is still considered to be the greatest exponent of the art of remodelling. His masterpiece, the Castelvecchio Museum in Verona, is composed of a complex of buildings, courtyards, gardens and the tower of the Scaliger Castle. It is situated beside a bridge that spans the River Adige, which runs through the centre of Verona.

The approach taken by Scarpa was one based upon an interpretation of the meaning of the original building. He endeavoured to understand the historical and contextual qualities of the place and then applied a new contemporary layer of value and consequence to the building. In response to the three main periods of the castle's history, the layers of building were scraped away and exposed until the junctions where time was most obvious were revealed. A new layer of small, beautifully composed additions were then imposed upon the building, a layer that expressed the contemporary nature of their design but which was totally appropriate and sympathetic to the original building.

Carlo Scarpa
Scarpa regarded himself as belonging to the Italian tradition of working with existing buildings, often citing the example of Brunelleschi, whose masterpiece, the dome of the Duomo in Florence, was an addition to an existing building.

'...Foster approaches restoration much as he does a specialist glazing or lift contract. He treats it as a discrete entity, to be handled by the people who know the subject best.'

Rowan Moore

Combined

Name:
Sackler Galleries,
Royal Academy of Arts

Location:
London, UK

Date:
1991

Designer:
Julian Harrap Architects,
Foster + Partners

A listed or precious building may be in particularly poor condition and therefore before any remodelling can be embarked upon, it must first undergo complete restoration.

In such cases, a combination of preservation, restoration, renovation or remodelling may be employed in unison; for example, when designing the Sackler Galleries at the Royal Academy of Arts in London, Foster + Partners ensured that the façades of the original buildings were completely restored by Julian Harrap Architects before embarking on the remodelling of the space.

The Sackler Galleries are accessed through what was once a narrow gap between the rear of the original building and the Garden House extension. Into this fine and slender slot of space, Foster + Partners have inserted a contrasting steel and glass circulation route. The original building is now viewed from a position that it had never been seen from before. The visitor can intimately examine the second- and third-storey windows from the new staircase and the new glass walls of the reception rest upon the cornice of Burlington House. The façades of the original building had to be restored with the same quality and expectations as the design of the brand new elements.

Above:
New and old
The new elements are inserted into the narrow gap between two buildings.

Left:
Circulation
The completely restored façades
sit quite comfortably with the new
modern insertion.

Below, left:
The foyer
The bright white reception
is placed at the top of the
existing lightwell.

Below:
The balcony
The visitor emerges into the
light of the foyer.

Above:
Reception
The meeting room provides
the backdrop for the reception.

Below:
The meeting room wall
The corrugated plastic
is recessed into the channel
at floor and ceiling level.

Below, right:
Concept sketch
of reorganisation
Openness and transparency
were the key design generators.

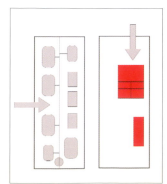

'The design process usually starts with a functional grouping of the parts...the trick is to investigate this grouping as much as possible.'

Peter Cook

Future function

Name:
Offices for the Architects
Registration Board (ARB)

Location:
London, UK

Date:
1999

Designer:
De Rijke Marsh Morgan Architects
(DRMM)

A highly influential factor within the process of the design of interiors is the consideration of the needs of the future users of the building or space. A firm understanding of the requirements, relationships and nature of the proposed function is needed if the designer is to provide adequate space or provision for the activities to take place within the interior. This understanding will also ensure that a strong relationship can be established between the old and the new when remodelling an existing building.

The Architects Registration Board asked for transparency and accessibility when their offices were redesigned. This was both a psychological and functional requirement and it formed the basis of the project. The designers created an open-plan office that afforded almost complete visual clarity, leaving only the meeting room and the service area enclosed. These private rooms are surrounded by a translucent polycarbonate wall, which actually glows when the room is occupied. The meeting room, which is situated in the centre of the space, forms the backdrop to the reception area. The translucent blue corrugated plastic wall has become part of the ARB logo, and has become symbolic of a new era of transparency in the organisation.

The most significant difference between the design of interiors and the design of almost anything else is the existence of the original building. The interior designer has to be forever conscious of the continual presence of an existing structure. But far from this being a handicap or constraining factor, it can be used as a valuable tool, an instrument of liberation. In the process of creating interior space, through the reworking of the existing building or given space, the stimulus for transformation can often be found in the existing building. This section will explain how the elements of the redesign can respond to the stimulus of the reading or analysis of the structure and rhythm of the existing building. The different methods of establishing a relationship between the new and old will be outlined and the significance of the important theory of remodelling, 'Form follows form', will be discussed.

Name:
Town Hall

Location:
Utrecht, the Netherlands

Date:
1999

Designer:
EMBT (Enric Miralles–Benedetta Tagliabue)

Reading the interior

A careful analysis of the space can offer many clues and pointers to the redesign. Understanding the plan, section and elevations of the building or space allows the designer to explore the relationships between the qualities of a space and its subsequent adaptation to a new use.

Basic structural systems

Thorough knowledge of structural issues can communicate the most practical methods of conversion and change, and avoid potentially dangerous construction problems. Rhythm, form and visual balance can also influence the subsequent issues of the remodelling.

Context & environment

All buildings have their own individual context and there are many considerations, both inside and outside, that can be manipulated and shaped within the reorganisation. Environmental issues need to be considered, not just problems of solar gain or stopping the rain from getting in, but also questions of the impact of any design upon the natural world.

History

An analysis of the existing building can expose features that may not be immediately discernible. Buildings evolve and develop over time; their original function will have determined their shape and form, their structural logic and their outward appearance. The previous users of the building will have affected its character – indeed, if it was designed for a particular use, then it will have a specific organisation. The new use may be completely different to their original purpose, yet an analysis of these features, their changes over time and their new functional requirements are important considerations. The analysis of growth and changes throughout the history of the building can offer some interesting clues to reuse.

Form follows form

It is through the understanding of the pre-existing that the remodelled building can become endowed with a new and greater meaning. An investigation of the archaeology of the original can reveal previously hidden or obsolete characteristics that contain the possibility of being exploited: the place can be activated.

Facing page:
New meets old in the interior of
St Paul's Church, Bow.

The reading of an existing building is a process that can be conducted in a series of methodical and distinct ways. This section will look at a number of analytical processes that the designer can adopt in order to understand the existing space.

Reading the plan

Name:
Marienkirche and Library

Location:
Muncheberg, Germany

Date:
1994

Designer:
Klaus Block

The drawn outline of a space or building indicates the parameters of the space to be used in the new design. This is described as the plan of the existing: it can be the meticulous survey of an existing building or a drawing of an as yet unbuilt structure. Understanding the extent of the plan of a space is an important part of the interior design process, as the drawing will indicate not only the exact area to be designed, but it can also provide information about the nature of the original building.

The reading of a plan of the existing building or new space can give clues to the distribution and nature of the function (both previous and proposed), the organisation, the structure and the rhythm of a space. Contextual features such as bays, windows and doorways are indicated in the drawings. The site plan also shows how the space or building is situated within its context. This drawing will indicate such factors as orientation, aspect, the relationship with neighbouring buildings, roads and public spaces.

This type of information is not always possible to fathom when visiting the site, and is near impossible if the building is unbuilt. It is these details that can give clues to the designer and influence the transformation of the space.

The reading of the surrounding envelope of the existing building has directly influenced the restoration of the Marienkirche in Muncheberg, Germany and the planning of the new town library. The body of the existing church was clearly organised into two distinct areas; the nave and the chancel. The congregation had dwindled so when the opportunity to combine the secular with the spiritual arose, it was obvious how the building should be split. The church retained the chancel and the library took over the nave. However, it was important that the two activities did not interfere with each other. The library is housed in an elegant timber and glass structure, reminiscent of the hull of a boat moored within the cavernous nave of the church. It is separated both visually and acoustically from the congregation, who pass through the space around the library to get to their seats. A free-standing lift services the library, clad with dark grey steel mesh, and perhaps seen as a modern interpretation of the Marienkirche's bell tower; an eighteenth-century addition by Karl Friedrich Schinkel.

The existing building

'…a building plan helps us see the stability and invention of a type, a single shift of perception transforms this concept into a matrix for interpreting the urban context and the principle of settlement that presides over it.'

Vittorio Gregotti

**Above:
Muncheberg Church
and Library**
View of the library from the chancel.

**Right, top to bottom:
Muncheberg Church
and Library**

Third floor plan.

Second floor plan.

First floor plan.

Ground floor plan.

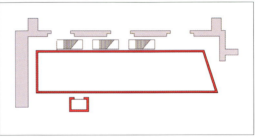

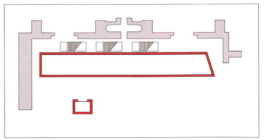

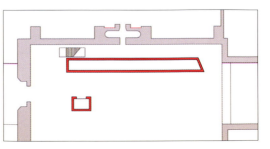

Reading the section

Name:
Fourth Church of Christ Scientist

Location:
Manchester, UK

Date:
1998

Designer:
OMI Architects

At any point on the plan of a building, the designer may describe a line through the drawing and visualise a vertical cut through the spaces. This is called a section and it will explain the volumes of the spaces and indicate the position of the walls, the floors, the roof and other structural elements. The building or space to be designed or reused can be read as a series of spaces and levels within an enclosure and this understanding allows the designer to respond to the existing forms and volumes. This type of drawing also allows the designer to investigate such issues as an exploration of the structure, the admission of light, vertical interaction within the building and relationships between the interior and the exterior.

The section allowed OMI to understand the volumetric properties of a banal office block in Manchester. Without this collection of drawings, they would not have been able to visually analyse the building so thoroughly, as complex three-dimensional relationships are not always obvious to the naked eye. This examination led the designers to carve from deep within the lower floors of the building a triple-height chapel. This large room or volume is surrounded by circulation space, through which shines natural light. At ground floor level, at the front of the building, the designers manipulated the barely double-height space to accommodate a reception and bookshop with a tiny reading room. A series of sections through the building provided the architects with a greater understanding of the building and this placed them in a position to develop complex relationships within the space.

Top:
The chapel
The structure of the existing building is emphasised to produce a subtle reference for the spiritual space.

Centre:
Church interior
Concept sketch.

Bottom:
Circulation
The message of the space is framed in the interior.

Below:
Section through the church
The space appears to be
carved from the heart of the
existing building.

'Every place has its datum-line, and one
may be on it or above it or below it.'

Gordon Cullen

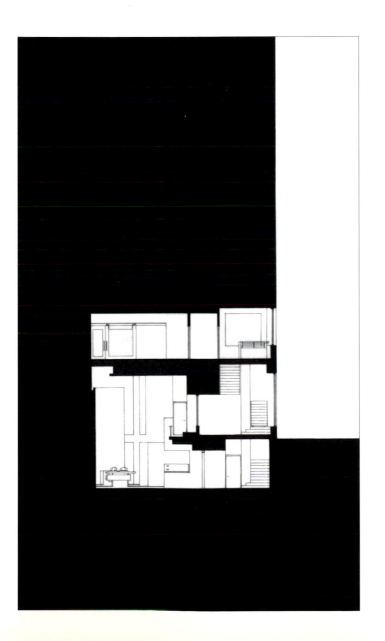

Above:
The new entrance
Black granite is placed against the gable end of the terrace.

Right:
The original Georgian façade
The relationship of the original buildings to the civic centre facilitated the re-orientation of the entrance façade.

The existing building

'The façade…talks about the cultural situation at the time when the building was built.'

Rob Krier

Reading the elevation

Name:
Henry Moore Institute

Location:
Leeds, UK

Date:
1993

Designer:
Dixon Jones

The elevation is a representation of the vertical plane of a building or space, thus the building elevation is a description of the outside walls, and an interior elevation is a description of the inside walls. The building elevation can give clues to the distribution of volumes and activities within the building and provide links with surrounding buildings or structures. The interior elevation will often describe a key part of the space and will invariably be stand-alone. It is sometimes difficult to differentiate between this and the section. The elevation shows pattern, order and proportion of the elements that make up the façade or wall. A façade is generally the main or principle or front elevation of the building. The analysis of the shape and form of the elevation, the openings, the structure and the logic, has an important impact on the organisation of a new design.

Analysis of the proportions of the façade of a building can provide the vocabulary for the design of new elements. In the extension to the Museum of Decorative Arts in Frankfurt, Germany, Richard Meier (see p.158) analysed the proportions of the original façade of the nineteenth-century town house and from an abstraction of this information, he derived the stark, pure, white modernist language of the new building.

It is not just the façade elevation of a building that can influence the new use. At the Henry Moore Gallery in Leeds, architects Dixon Jones have reused a terrace of Georgian townhouses to create galleries and a study centre for artists' work. The main elevations of the houses in front of a narrow street are untouched, while the gable end of the terrace, facing the civic centre of Leeds, is appropriated to become the new entrance. The cultural context of the site and the new role for the buildings has provided the impetus for the enigmatic, crenulated black granite face. The recessed entrance is placed in the centre of the vertical black plane and serves to further accentuate the monolithic qualities of the new façade.

Above:
New and old
3-D drawing showing the relationship between the plane of black granite and the terrace.

'...it would be difficult to name any internationally recognised architect without making a reference to their drawing style.'

Tom Porter

Above:
Museum façade
The modest neo-classical exterior has been sensitively altered.

Three-dimensional form

Name:
German Museum of Architecture

Location:
Frankfurt, Germany

Date:
1984

Designer:
O.M. Ungers

The plan, section and elevation of a building can all be read together to provide information about the three-dimensional qualities of the building. The plan will show the extent of a space, while the section will show the height, and combined they will indicate the volume. These orthographic drawings are diagrams that aid the designer's understanding of a building or space, but it is the three-dimensional qualities that are seen, felt, heard and experienced. From this analysis, the volume and form can be established and subsequently considered in the design process.

Frankfurt has pursued a policy of regeneration through culture by redeveloping the south bank of the river Main with a series of museums. As part of this development O.M. Ungers has created an extraordinary museum within the confines of an existing building. The modest exterior of the neo-classical townhouse has been wrapped with an equally reserved single-storey, red sandstone colonnade; but it is within the museum that the true extent of the remodelling can be experienced. Ungers has inserted a huge white representation of a house into the cleared interior of the building – 'a house within a house'. This element controls and defines the extent of the exhibitions and can be accessed from every floor. A powerful three-dimensional grid defines the position and size of the house. From the entrance hall, four columns direct the eye upwards and the sheer size of this clean, white element is obvious through the void of the empty space. It is a very powerful gesture, a post-modern, almost ironic symbol of architecture.

Above:
Interior
A house within a house.

Right:
Axonometric of the project
The new structure sits completely
within the old one.

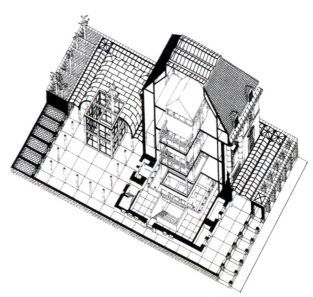

This section will examine the different basic structural systems and the types of interior that can be created from them. It will examine the qualities of interiors designed as a result of understanding and using these systems.

What is structure?

Structure can be described as a collection or assemblage of materials that, when joined together, will withstand the loads and forces to which they are subjected. These loads are not confined just to the weight of the building itself, but will also include such forces as wind, people, furniture and fittings. The interior designer needs to have an understanding of structure in order to be sure that any alterations or additions that they make to an existing building will not compromise its structural integrity.

Up until the end of the twentieth century there were two basic methods of construction: load-bearing and frame. The load-bearing structure is thick and heavy and is usually constructed from bricks or stone blocks built up from the ground. This type of structure generally creates small confined spaces due to the restricted span of the roof or floor beams, and the windows are of a limited size. The frame structure is constructed from a series of columns and beams, usually organised in a grid formation, which take the weight of the building. They can be made from concrete, steel or timber. This creates large open spaces. The walls, which take no structural load, can be divorced from the structure and so the choice of cladding material is almost unlimited. This type of organisation is referred to as free-plan. The twenty-first century has brought contemporary methods of construction, such as monocoques and fractals, and has seen the resurgence of barrel vaulting.

The structural logic of an existing building is a key factor that will influence the remodelling. Different types and qualities of space can be created from different structural systems. This understanding is a key part of the reading and analysis of the building.

Facing page:
New and old
The steel-framed restaurant and shops are inserted into the brick and timber structure of the Great Butchers' Hall (Groentenmarkt) in Ghent.

The existing building

Load bearing

Name:
Scottish Poetry Library

Location:
Edinburgh, Scotland

Date:
1999

Designer:
Malcolm Fraser Architects

Load-bearing buildings contain thick walls, constructed using stone or brick and are built up from the ground, layer by layer, incorporating their own weight. The organisation of the building and its spaces can be very random, although there is a constraint upon the size of the spaces created; they can be positioned without any considerations for order, rhythm or control. There is generally a limit to the height of the building: the walls at the base become ridiculously wide should the building become too high. The restriction upon the volume of the individual rooms is caused by the difficulty of spanning the space; wood and steel beams are generally of a limited length. Victorian buildings combined cast-iron columns with brick outer walls to accommodate the need for large uninterrupted spaces. Openings in the walls have to ensure that they do not compromise the structural integrity of the building, so they tend to be quite small and aligned. The top is supported by an arch or lintel.

The reuse of load-bearing buildings usually results in a very specific type of interior architecture: small confined spaces with relatively restricted natural light. Any structural changes have to be thoroughly compensated for. This was the most common building technique before the nineteenth century and as a consequence will often be the subject of a remodelling project.

The Scottish Poetry Library is partially built upon the old city wall that surrounded Edinburgh. It uses the wall as a protective container that also supports the roof at the rear of the library. The front of the building is a modern steel, timber and glass construction. The original arrow slit eyelet windows of the city wall illuminate the gaps between the bookshelves, thus a book is selected from the protective shadowy depths of the building and brought into the light.

Above:
Poetry library
Books are selected within the depths of the building.

Facing page top:
Sectional Perspective
The building sits on the city wall at the back and opens up to the landscape at the front.

Facing page bottom:
The library in context
The open-stepped terrace for reading is clearly visible at the front of the building.

Malcolm Fraser Architects
Malcolm Fraser Architects are recognised for their sympathetic and contextual approach to architecture and the remodelling of buildings in sensitive and historic environments. As well as the Scottish Poetry Library, they have successfully reused buildings for Dance Base and the Scottish Storytelling Centre.

The existing building

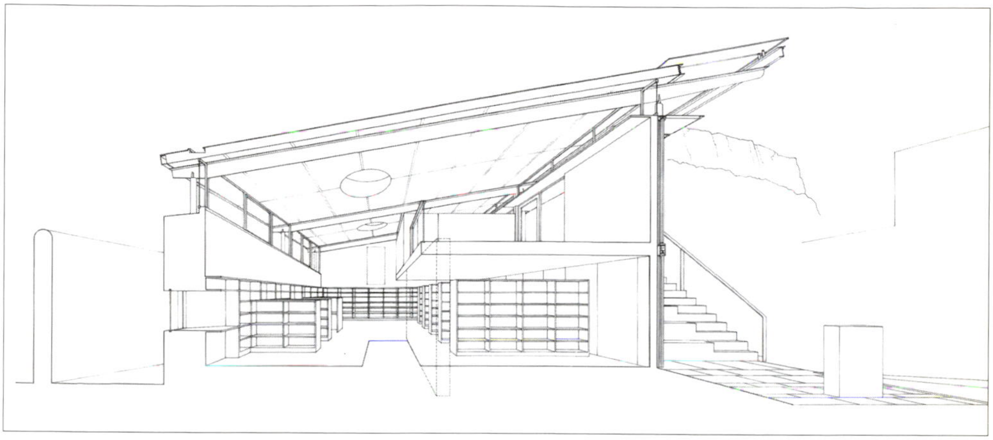

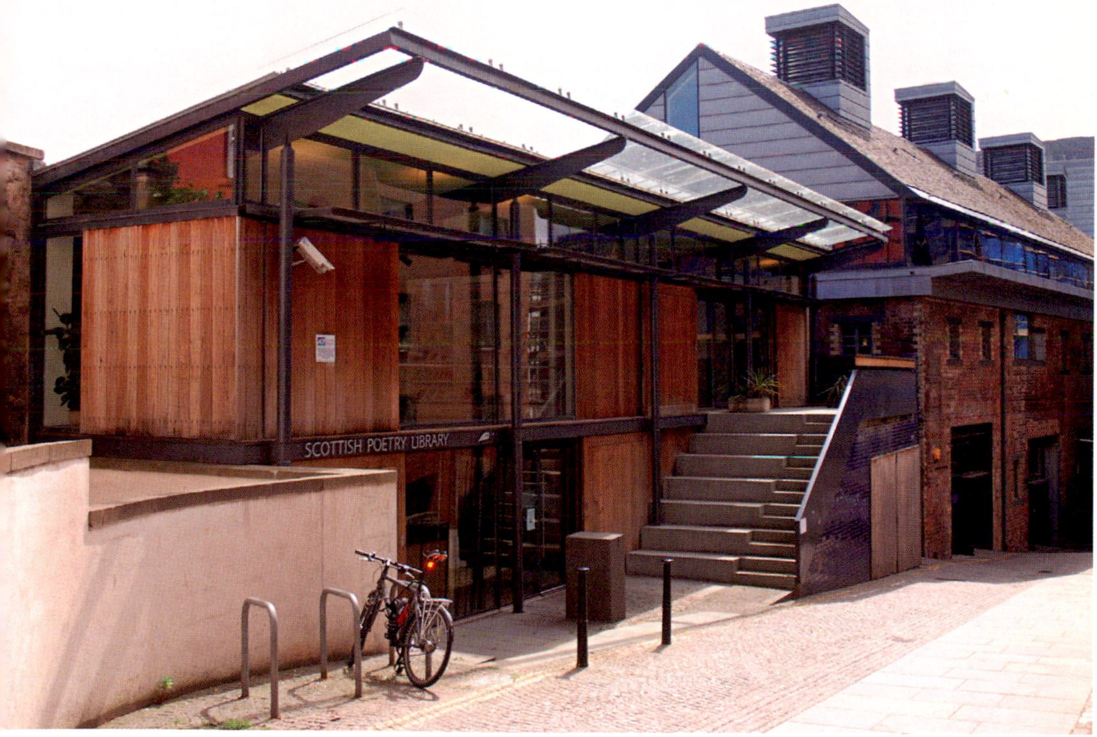
SCOTTISH POETRY LIBRARY

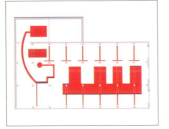

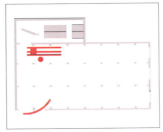

Above:
Circulation
The frame of the building dictates
the position of the stairs.

Left:
Plans
First floor and ground floor plans.

Facing page, left:
The upper level balcony
Within the original building there
is a progression of different types
of space.

Facing page, right:
The attic
The rhythm of the building
structure is visible on the top floor,
which is awaiting remodelling.

Enric Miralles

Enric Miralles was the architect for the Scottish
Parliament, an extraordinary and dynamic building,
apparently based on an upturned boat. His vibrant
and free buildings utilised massive building materials
and were rooted in their context, having a very
direct relationship with their immediate environment.

The existing building

Frame

Name:
La Llauna School

Location:
Barcelona, Spain

Date:
1986

Designer:
Enric Miralles and Carme Pinós

A building with a frame construction usually has a definite order to it. The columns are generally arranged as a grid, leaving free, uninterrupted space between them. The frame is usually made from steel, concrete or timber. The floors are generally in-filled between the beams of the frame and, as such, they will have a limited ability to take weight. When Jakob & Macfarlane designed the Restaurant Georges in the Pompidou Centre (see p.138), they had to be very conscious of the thin concrete slab floors.

The walls within and surrounding the building can be thin, as they do not have to correspond to the frame; this is described as free-plan. They can be arranged into any pattern or organisation that will support the activity of the building. The choice of material for the internal walls and cladding is also almost unlimited. They only have to support themselves; they take no structural load and so can be constructed with consideration to other factors, such as acoustic control, visual impact or organisation. The external walls or cladding are also non-structural, but environmental control will be an important factor in their design. Keeping the rain out, preventing excessive solar gain and providing acoustic and visual privacy are important considerations. However, this is not always the case: Blur Pavilion, designed by Diller Scofidio + Renfro for the 2002 Expo in Switzerland, used steam from hundreds of sprinklers to surround and define the building.

For La Llauna School, Miralles and Pinós used the structural logic of a disused printing warehouse to inform the organisation of the new school that was placed within it. The classrooms, staff rooms, circulation and even the playground are positioned with consideration for the steel frame structure. A series of architectural interventions were slipped between the structure; the stairs rise through a vertical slot of space and open a route through the building, classrooms are placed in-between the grid of columns, and at ground level all superfluous elements have been stripped away to leave just the frame, thus creating an open yet sheltered area for the children's playground. The small school, built on an incredibly constrained site, is an elegant and distinct conversation between new and old.

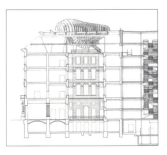

Unusual structures

Name:
ING & NNH Head Offices

Location:
Budapest, Hungary

Date:
1997

Designer:
Erick van Egeraat (EEA)

As well as straightforward frame and load-bearing structure systems, there is a more unusual method of construction. With the advent of three-dimensional modelling software, designers can now create seamless structures that combine the walls, floors and the roof of a building.

The fractal geometries of Frank Gehry and Daniel Libeskind produce complex geometries that twist and turn to produce contorted interior spaces. Monocoque constructions such as the media centre at Lord's cricket ground in London by Future Systems, are similar in construction to the hulls of boats and distort the usual relationships between floors, walls and ceilings. Foreign Office Architects have designed a series of projects that are little more than undulating landscapes, where the traditional thresholds between inside and outside have been blurred.

Eric van Egeraat has added a dramatic and provocative element to a sober neo-Renaissance building that was designed in 1882 in the centre of Budapest. The orthogonal five-storey building is arranged around a full height courtyard and is elegantly ordered with cast-iron balconies and windows. The protected building was painstakingly restored, any lost details of the ornament were reconstructed and the destroyed and damaged fabric was cleaned and repaired. It was important that any new additions were not visible from the street so accordingly, it was within the courtyard that the insertion was placed.

Set into the roof of the building and hovering over the courtyard is a new double-height structure with a translucent green glass underside. Known locally as 'the whale', this large monocoque construction functions as a viewing platform and meeting room. Egeraat describes the strategy as 'modern baroque', prioritising the roof or ceiling of a space and ensuring that the visitor looks up as they enter:

'In that modern baroque, it is essential to leave symmetry and structure behind and instead introduce asymmetry and disharmony, freed from its negative connotations. I am above all obsessed with the excitement one feels in all that is indefinable and inexplicable.'[1]

1
Van Egeraat, E. 1997.
EEA Six Ideas about Architecture.
New York: Birkhäuser

Facing page left:
Roof top view
'The whale' sits on top of the roof
of the neo-Renaissance building.

Facing page right:
Section through the building
The boardroom is suspended
above the internal courtyard.

Left:
The roof
The meeting room emerges
from its glass surrounds.

Below left:
**View from the top of the
circulation route**
Large rectangular windows
allow light and views into the
meeting room.

Below:
Inside 'the whale'
The enigmatic space
of the boardroom.

Rhythm

Name:
Alte Pinakothek

Location:
Munich, Germany

Date:
1952

Designer:
Hans Döllgast

The structural system of a building can help create an order or rhythm. This may be little more than a sequence of identical windows, or perhaps an ornate covered colonnade. A procession of repeated elements can tie long buildings together and can also compensate for any discrepancies within the building. Palladio used a rhythm of columns and arches to wrap around the Basilica in Vicenza, Italy (see p.154). This acted to conceal the distorted shape of the interior building.

The Alte Pinakothek was designed in 1836 by Leo von Klenze as part of King Ludwig I of Bavaria's ambition to turn Munich into the Venice of the North. The central section of the neo-Classical building was destroyed during the Second World War. The design for the restoration of the Pinakothek was not only modern but it also managed to reflect the rhythm and tempo of the original building. The 19-metre-high brick piers that had been destroyed were replaced with 250mm steel columns. New sections of the roof were formed in aluminium and the brick wall was reinstated, but in a more simple and austere manner. This gives the foyer space a minimal and modern quality, while the remodelling of the exterior appears to be appropriate without resorting to pastiche.

Döllgast appreciated that the building had a history, and he felt it important to recognise and respect this. The reinstatement of the rhythm and order of the original building ensured that there was a direct connection between the new and the old.

Top:
Elevation
The repaired section is
celebrated. The rhythm of the
old dictates the new.

Left:
Detail of the façade
The difference between the
language of the old and the new
is clearly visible at the point at
which they meet.

Hans Döllgast
Hans Döllgast was much admired for his inventive
use of modernist principles in the conservation
of historic buildings. As well as the Pinakothek,
he designed two modern roof structures for
war-damaged churches in Munich, St. Bonifaz and
Allerheilgenhof. Both structures are sympathetic
to the existing building and yet are still modern
and uncompromising.

Above:
New and old
The new extension makes
direct reference to the character
of the original building.

The existing building

Form/balance

Name:
Gothenburg Law Courts

Location:
Gothenburg, Sweden

Date:
1937

Designer:
Erik Gunnar Asplund

The form of the original building can motivate or generate the form of an extension or insertion. Certain particular characteristics can inspire the new design or remodelling. In sites of historical sensitivity, issues of continuity and tradition are key to regeneration. Embodied meaning within an existing building can be analysed and interpreted to create new architecture and design.

The classical law courts in Gothenburg were substantially constructed in 1817 by B.W. Carlberg and are located in the centre of old Gothenburg, the principal elevation facing onto Gustav Adolfs Torg. The extension by Asplund is sensitively modest; it doesn't overpower the original façade, but rather supports and even defers to it. The new façade is itself asymmetrically modern, but it does employ the proportions and rhythm of the original building. A slight recess separates the two, but the height of the building and the position and proportions of the windows remain constant. The colour scheme of the original building is replicated, white for structure and yellow for infill, and the important rooms on the first floor have enlarged windows with decorated reliefs above. All of the windows are positioned to the left of the grid, so that they appear to acknowledge and respect the original building. The extension completes the internal courtyard and thus creates a balanced interior. The law courts are a careful composition of old and new.

Erik Gunnar Asplund
Erik Gunnar Asplund is generally considered to be Sweden's leading architect. He designed, with Sigurd Lewerentz, the Woodland Cemetery in Stockholm, creating the elegantly modern Crematorium and the more rustic Woodland Chapel. He is probably best known for Stockholm City Library, a classical cylinder within a square.

'Context & environment' will examine the impact that the surroundings of a building can have upon its redesign. It will also discuss such environmental considerations as topography and light.

Context: site

Name:
CCCB (Centre de Cultura Contemporánia de Barcelona)

Location:
Barcelona, Spain

Date:
1993

Designer:
Albert Viaplana, Helio Piñon

The exterior context around an interior can be an important and influential consideration. There are many site-specific situations that influence the shape and form of a building and subsequently have an effect on the design of its interior. Such contextual factors can include aspect, orientation, topography, the patterns of street and roads, urban density, and the relationship with a significant landmark.

Above:
The screen
The world beyond the courtyard is reflected in the angled screen.

The CCCB is housed in an elegant eighteenth-century building arranged around a courtyard. Around three sides of the courtyard, the Casa de Caritat (the Almshouse), a four-storey building with basements, was retained, and on the fourth side the building was demolished and a new insertion was placed within this gap. It was built to fit, adhering to the exact plan dimensions of its predecessor. The courtyard façade of the new building is a striking glazed screen that is angled at the top as it rises over the rooftops of the other buildings. The main circulation routes are secreted behind this screen, but it is in front of it that the most significant moment of the building is discovered. The glazed screen is highly reflective, offering mirror images of the buildings and the courtyard. But when the visitor is positioned upon a specific bench on the far side of the courtyard, the angled screen provides a view over the roofscape to the sea. Immediately a relationship is established with things both close up and far away.

'The relationship between the object and the intervening spaces is not formal: it is always rooted in the context of a particular setting.'

Dalibor Vesely

Above:
Old meets new
The screen is inserted into the courtyard.

Right:
Section through the courtyard
The screen defines the fourth edge of the courtyard.

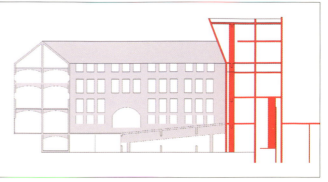

Context: exterior

Name:
The Brasserie

Location:
Manhattan, New York

Date:
2000

Designer:
Diller + Scofidio

Important contextual factors do not only shape the exterior of the building but can also exert great influence upon the interior. Although the location, scale, size and shape of an existing building can influence the reuse, psychological factors can also have a significant effect.

Ludwig Mies van de Rohe designed the Seagram Building in New York in 1959. It is the archetypical international style building, a symbol of modernity's obsession with right-angles, overt structure and truth to materials. This is expressed in the sleek curtain wall of smoked glass and the exposed bronze structure. The Seagram was notable for the fact that it did not fill its expansive Park Avenue lot to the perimeter. Instead the architect set the building back from the road on a travertine plinth, almost a piece of sculpture set apart from its neighbours. Within the basement of the plinth was the fashionable Four Seasons Restaurant. This was designed by Philip Johnson, who was exclusively and extensively responsible for everything, right down to the napkins. After a very destructive fire, the restaurant was remodelled by Diller + Scofidio in 2000. The context provoked a response based upon the contradictions of the immediate environment: a basement location without a view of the outside world, which was situated in the bottom of an iconic example of transparency and light. Therefore the Brasserie is conceived around the concept, of watching and being watched. The diner is observed twice: firstly, upon entrance their image is relayed to one of a series of screens suspended above the bar and then again, when they enter the catwalk-type staircase into the dining area – an experience that is not for the shy or fainthearted.

Philip Johnson
Philip Johnson (1906–2005) was one of the twentieth century's most influential architects. His early career included working with a number of eminent modernist architects, including Mies van der Rohe, Le Corbusier and Walter Gropius. His own masterpiece, the Glass House (1949) was a composition in minimalism and transparency. In a complete rejection of this style, he designed, in 1984, what has been described as the first post-modern building, the AT&T Building.

Above:
The dining room
The space is conceived
as a series of eating and
drinking experiences.

Facing page:
Seagram plaza
The restaurant is located within
the basement plinth.

Right:
The restaurant
Images of the visitors are
displayed on screens above
the bar.

Below:
Under surveillance
A concept sketch of the interior.

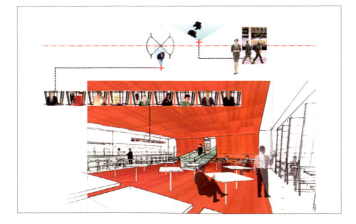

'Light is not so much something that reveals, as it is itself the revelation.'

James Turrell

Above:
By day
The building is undistinguished.

Right:
By night
The façade is animated through light.

Below left:
The foyer
Idiosyncratic furniture and enigmatic objects are crammed into the space.

Below right:
The restaurant
Colour and atmosphere is created by the columns, which have been wrapped with bookshelves.

Context: artificial light

Name:
St Martins Lane Hotel

Location:
London, UK

Date:
2000

Designer:
Philippe Starck

Artificial light can be regarded as a material with definite properties that can be refined and manipulated. The artist James Turrell has created a series of installations, all of which exploit the deceptive possibilities that bright light, and its opposite, extreme dark, can offer. Artificial light is of course most visible at night, or in a space undisturbed by natural light.

In the heart of London's West End, a 1960s modernist block, the former home of a major advertising agency, has been transformed to become an exclusive boutique hotel. Within the interior, Starck employs his usual wit in the design of a post-modern collection of magnified and classically inspired furniture. Each space is radically different, the Light Bar is vivid and brightly coloured, the lobby is cool, spacious and white, with a ten-foot high vase of flowers and massive representations of gold teeth and corks acting as cocktail chairs and tables, the Asia de Cuba & Rum Bar contains a tight grid of tiny tables tottering on tall slender legs and the outrageously large columns in the restaurant are enclosed with bookshelves and picture walls – an ironic interpretation of the family living room?

However, Starck reserves his most extravagant gesture for the exterior of the building. The outside walls of the fairly anonymous office block have a visible structural concrete grid and floor to ceiling glazing. Stark exploits this transparency: by day, the hotel retains its undistinguished character, but at night each room glows with coloured light and thus the building is transformed into a bright and glowing patchwork. The guests control the colour and intensity of the light, they can select the colour that they feel most reflects their emotion, offering the passing pedestrian a hint of what is happening behind the net curtains.

Left:
The Light Bar
Vivid coloured light illuminates the space.

Context: sustainability

Name:
Greenpeace Headquarters

Location:
London, UK

Date:
1990

Designer:
Feilden Clegg Bradley Architects

It is very environmentally friendly to re-use existing buildings, simply because the massive amount of energy required to build new, in both the materials and the man power does not have to be expended. It is of an even greater benefit if the conversion is made using sustainable techniques. The designer can select materials that do not contain huge amounts of embodied energy, that have been sourced locally and that do not harbour toxic or hazardous chemicals. Additionally, remodelling can be made more environmentally sound by considering how the building is used. It can be designed so that the minimum amount of energy is expended in the day-to-day use and so that the environment that is created is beneficial to everyone who occupies it.

Feilden Clegg Bradley Architects converted a 1920s factory and office building into the headquarters for Greenpeace UK. This presented a number of difficult problems for the architects. Greenpeace wanted to minimise CO_2 emissions, to remove as far as possible any factor that might contribute to 'sick building syndrome' and to reduce the environmental impact of the various materials used. The project makes maximum use of the considerable window area, for the access of both natural light and ventilation. Pivoting screens fixed at the point of the external walls act in two ways to control the levels of sunlight entering the building.

Firstly, as sunlight enters the building it is bounced at high level off the pivoting reflectors, across the room to reflect again from natural cotton ceiling-mounted canopies and into the centre of the deep office. The pivoting screens also stop any direct penetration of natural light into the building by acting as louvres on the exterior of the building. Small casements at the top and bottom of the windows open; this encourages cross-ventilation and the movement of clean air into the depths of the building. The centrally placed open stair admits natural light into the centre of the building and aids ventilation by encouraging the stack effect. Greenpeace needed to make a statement about the environmental possibilities of re-using an existing building, Feilden Clegg Bradley fulfilled all their expectations.

Facing page:
Section through the office
The room is naturally lit
and ventilated.

Below:
Interior views
The offices are constructed from
a collection of carefully selected
and sustainable materials.

'Green design is place sensitive. One of its attractions
in a globalising world is the potential to make
place-specific architecture by responding to the clues
of a specific climate and site, and, where possible,
using sustainable local materials.'

The Energy Research Group

The history of an existing building can be analysed and the findings can influence the subsequent redesign. This section will examine the use of history as a transformative tool in the redesign process.

Top:
Entrance façade
Large quantities of natural light are admitted into the gallery.

Above:
Riverside elevation
The insertion of the new gallery has reinforced the iconic quality of the building.

'The most sympathetic and stimulating places in which
to see modern contemporary art are in older buildings
converted from earlier industrial uses or other purposes.'

Iwona Blazwick & Simon Wilson (eds)

History: Focus study 1

Name:
BALTIC

Location:
Gateshead, England

Date:
2002

Designer:
Ellis Williams Architects

The previous function of
a building can have an enormous
impact upon its redesign. The
original building was constructed
for a specific use, and traces
of this will inevitably be present
when it is remodelled. Whether
a factory with large open spaces
or a dwelling with small rooms,
the specific use for which the
building was designed will have
determined the size, shape and
hence the form of the space.
The designer has the opportunity
to reflect upon the contingency,
usefulness and emotional
resonance of particular places
and structures.

BALTIC art gallery, on the banks
of the Tyne river in Gateshead
in north-east of England, is
contained within the once
magnificent and iconic Baltic
Flour Mill. The building was
originally constructed as a series
of massive concrete flour silos
or storage containers, which were
placed within the area defined
by four even larger towers. These
gave structural stability to the
building. The architects removed
the silos and placed the museum
within the vacant space. Columns
were inset from the perimeter
walls, to create as much free
space as possible and beams
were slung between them to
support the six levels of gallery
space. Circulation was placed
within the retained towers. The
two short and now empty ends
of the building were glazed,
allowing large amounts of natural
light to penetrate into the interior
spaces. A large Teflon sail was
positioned over the eastern end
to offer protection from excessive
solar gain. The enormous flour
mill lettering on the sides of the
building was retained, a reminder
of the once magnificent days
of the industrial port.

Above:
New and old
Three-dimensional sketch
of the building.

History: Focus study 2

Name:
Rivoli Museum of
Contemporary Art

Location:
Rivoli, near Turin, Italy

Date:
1985

Designer:
Andrea Bruno Architects

A building can evolve, but it can retain a remembrance of its former function and value; it has a memory of its previous purpose ingrained within its very structure. The exploitation and development of this can create a composite of meaning and consequence. The inherent qualities of the place and its surroundings, combined with the anticipation of the future use, produce a multi-layered complexity impossible to replicate in a new building. The study or analysis of individual structure is almost an archaeological investigation. The history and changing function of a building is a valuable narrative that can be analysed and then used in the transformation process.

Andrea Bruno was commissioned to convert the Castello di Rivoli, (which had originally been built for the Savoy family by Filippo Juvarra), into the Museum of Contemporary Art. His careful and thorough analysis of the site revealed not one building, but several distinct layers of buildings from different eras. The elegant but unfinished eighteenth-century house was built upon the ruins of a seventeenth-century palace that had been constructed on top of a sixteenth-century castle, which itself was built over medieval ruins. Each layer was not fully demolished before the successive building was constructed, hence Bruno discovered that the site contained half of an eighteenth-century palace, an incredibly long seventeenth-century picture gallery and just some remains of the older buildings. Bruno's approach was to celebrate this diversity and to stitch these individual and distinctive elements together with a series of obviously modern interventions. Apart from the new roof for the picture gallery, the additions facilitated movement through and around the site. This encouraged the visitor to examine the buildings with the same scrutiny as the art. No attempt was made to physically connect the buildings, but a small balcony was cantilevered from the chateau to provide a visual link, thus allowing the visitor to make their own connection. Bruno has thus created another layer of archaeology that ties together the collage of the museum.

Top:
Old and new
The viewing balcony projects from the original building.

Above:
Vertical circulation
The new stairs are inserted into the old stairwell.

The existing building

'…when the organisational geometries do not reside in the objects themselves, the possibilities of combining various buildings within a system of order which attributes to each piece a bit of the of the organisation become almost infinite.'

Thomas Schumacher

Left:
Ariel view of the site
The long gallery after remodelling.

Below:
Architect's plan
Bruno's drawing of the new gallery on top of the existing buildings.

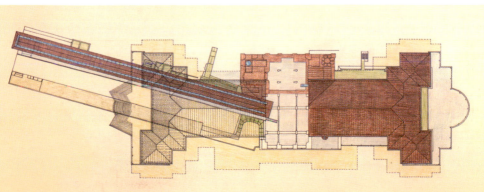

There are many methods of adapting old buildings for new uses. The qualities found within the existing can be a highly influential factor within the redesign process. The form of the existing can inform the form of the new.

Form follows form: Focus study 1

Name:
St Paul's Church, Bow

Location:
London, UK

Date:
2004

Designer:
Matthew Lloyd Architects

When a building is renewed or remodelled, the most important consideration is the nature of that building. For the design to be both sympathetic and appropriate, the designer must be able to appreciate the qualities of the existing. The form of the building will inevitably influence the form of the new interior, because it is itself the material that is to be altered or changed.

The church at Bow is a collection of assorted elements gathered together in one building. It is modestly gothic (1878), with a cylindrical three-storey bell tower, very large pointed windows and clerestory lights and an open nave. The ceiling over the chancel is highly decorated, the gold ribs run into the cast-iron columns, which are positioned centrally in front of pilasters between the windows. It appears that the brick walls of the nave were once painted white, but these have been allowed to peel and fade. The pews are placed around the raised altar and the organ is positioned against a blocked up arch. Into this mixture Matthew Lloyd Architects have inserted a two-storey steel and timber structure. It is raised high into the vaulted ceiling of the church to leave the chancel and the nave free for worship.

The front of this bold, curved wooden structure is supported by four enormous white painted Y-shaped steel columns, which just stand among the pews. The rear is connected to a white rectangular box of a quite different nature, and contained within this is the meeting room and stairs to the gallery, gym, and community rooms at first and second levels. The building has been split three-dimensionally into two L-shaped sections. The church occupies the L at the front and ground level and the community use the L at the top and back of the building. The language of the new is quite different to that of the old, but then each area is an assemblage of different styles, components and functions, the solution of which seems to work.

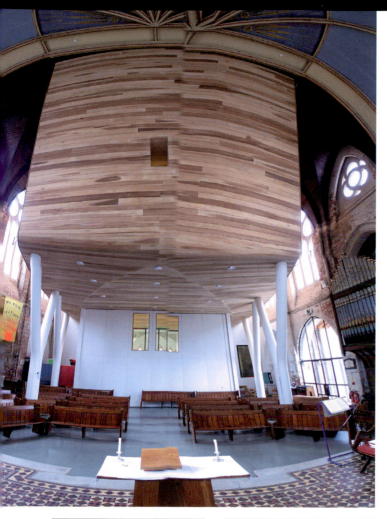

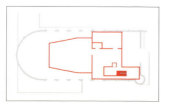

Above:
View from the altar
The new insertion is squeezed into the nave of the church.

Left:
Solid and void
Three-dimensional drawing of the new insertion and the old building.

Bottom left:
New and old
Plan of the project.

Top:
A collection of objects
There is a balance between the language of the new and the old.

Above:
The 'Y' shaped columns that support the community centre
The uncompromising modern structure of the insertion is balanced by the robust brickwork of the church.

Above:
The open roof
The balcony is squeezed into the open roof structure.

Right:
Threshold
The new elements are arranged around the structure of the existing building.

Far right:
Circulation
The stairs occupy a vertical shaft that cuts through the building.

'The La Llauna school threads a narrative at the human scale, a *promenade architecturale*, throughout the site, and thus transforms it by a change of scale and a degree of tactility. The school is about everything except classrooms.'

Josep Maria Montaner

Form follows form: Focus study 2

Name:
La Llauna School

Location:
Barcelona, Spain

Date:
1986

Designer:
Enric Miralles and Carme Pinós

A series of selective interventions can accentuate the character of a place while facilitating the new functions that will be situated within it. This was the approach taken at the La Llauna School in a suburb of Barcelona. The form of the existing building exerted a great influence upon the form of the remodelling and therefore upon the design of the new school. This was not just the structure but also the quality of light and space that existed within and around the building.

The approach that Miralles and Pinós took to the remodelling of an old factory in Barcelona was to exploit all the qualities of the existing building. The factory was typical of industrial buildings constructed at the end of the nineteenth century: brick outer walls with cast-iron columns inside and tied together with lattice beams. A school needs certain basic amenities, the main hall, classrooms, services and a playground. Here the existing building occupied a very tight position within a congested and dense urban area. It was completely enclosed within the crowded context; there was not even open exterior space available for the children to play in.

The architects carved an open space from the ground floor, thus releasing the recreational area. The structural columns did prove to be problematic; they couldn't be removed, so several of the most dangerous have been wrapped with brightly coloured foam. The cut slots of vertical circulation allow natural light to filter through the building and linger at ground level. Alterations to the main entrance of the school signalled the change of use, part of the front wall was removed and a new glazed structure including an enormous curved sliding door was inserted. This functionally allowed the large number of students access, but also acted as a statement of the new language. The basic nature of the building was retained, selective cuts and additions exploited and accentuated these qualities while inserting a new function into and around the existing spaces.

In building construction there are two predominant structure systems: load bearing and frames, as discussed in the first chapter. These approaches lead to quite different types of spaces. Load-bearing masonry walls create small, contained rooms with openings of a limited size, while the structural frame provides the space with freedom, as the walls do not have to correspond to the position of the columns. This chapter will explore both the closed room and the free plan by examining precedents from designers who have approached the creative process using similar techniques. These methods are: symmetry, asymmetry, balance, rhythm, playstation and addition.

Name:
Unity Chapel

Location:
Oak Park, Chicago

Date:
1904

Designer:
Frank Lloyd Wright

'Loos's Raumplan reached its apotheosis in his last domestic works, the Moller and Müller houses of 1928 and 1930… both these works are organised about displacements in the respective levels of their principle floors, elisions that serve not only to create spatial movement but also to differentiate one living area from the next… at a domestic level (Loos) gave primacy to the sensation of space rather then the revelation of architectonic structure.'

Kenneth Frampton

Closed room

The compact and contained space created by the load-bearing system is best exemplified in the work of Adolf Loos (1870–1933). Within the design of a series of houses in Vienna, he explored the quality and ordering of three-dimensional space and its relationship with the exterior. He referred to these tight and expressive spaces as 'Raumplan'.

Right:
Tristan Tzara House, Paris, by Adolf Loos.

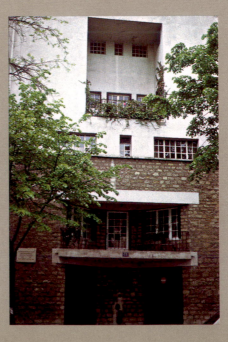

'The 5 points of a New Architecture by Le Corbusier and Pierre Jeanneret are:

1
The Column (les pilotis)

2
The Roof Garden (les troits jardins)

3
The Free Plan (le plan libre)

4
The Ribbon Window (la fenetre en longueur)

5
The Free Façade (La Façade libre)

The Free plan is usually taken as the focal point of these 5 points, introducing what was an essentially new architecture, one which develops from the inside towards the outside.'

Arjan Hebly

Free plan

The open freedom of the framed structure was exploited by Le Corbusier (1887–1965), who explored the modernist possibilities of embracing new technology, liberty and importance of function. This was referred to as 'Plan Libre' or free plan, which was at the heart of his Five Points of Architecture.

Right:
Villa Savoye, Poissy, by Le Corbusier.

This section will explore the concept of space as a series of closed inter-related rooms. The organisation of these rooms is directly influenced by the nature of the structure of the building and the materials used in its construction.

Symmetry

Name:
Villa Rotonda

Location:
Vicenza, Italy

Date:
1566

Designer:
Andrea Palladio

The Villa Rotonda is a good example of a symmetrical building; not just due to the classical style of architecture, but also as a consequence of its context. The building is situated at the top of a small, gently sloping hill. The villa and the landscape are intertwined; the rise of the hill becomes the steps of the building. The building has four identical façades, because it has views in all directions. These portico entrances lead to a circular central hall, which is highly decorated and top lit from the roof lights in the dome. The plan of the building shows four main lines of reflective symmetry, but the function has been compromised by this desire for balance and proportion. The shape and scale of the individual rooms is dictated by the harmonious arrangement of the dominant façades and round central space.

Top:
Villa Rotonda
The villa sits on the brow of the hill.

Above:
The approach
The framed view from the entrance gate of the approach to the villa.

Above:
Vista
View from within the portico, out to the landscape.

'The place is nicely situated and one of the loveliest and most charming that one could find; for it lies on the slopes of a hill, which is very easy to reach. The loveliest hills are arranged around it, and afford a view into an immense theatre…Because one takes pleasure in the beautiful views on all four sides, loggias were built on all four façades.'

Palladio, Wundram, Pape, Martin

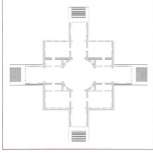

Above:
View of the interior
The magnificent internal rotonda.

Left:
Plan of the house
The plan is a *tour de force* of symmetry.

'Pierre Hebbelinck's restoration is simultaneously respectful and subversive.'

Maurizio Cohen

Asymmetry

Name:
Museum of Contemporary Art (MAC's)

Location:
Grand Hornu, Belgium

Date:
2002

Designer:
Pierre Hebbelinck

Enclosed spaces need not be balanced or symmetrical; neither do they need to be arranged in an ordered manner. There are many opportunities for contradiction and distinction in remodelling, when the elements are positioned in an irregular arrangement and contrasted with a balanced original organisation.

Le Grand Hornu, a neo-classical-style mining complex near Mons in Belgium, was built by the French-born industrialist, Henri de Gorge in the first half of the nineteenth century. The buildings of the colliery are built around a magnificent courtyard and include warehouses, stables, iron and brass foundries, coke-fired furnaces and engineers' offices. Hebbelinck has introduced a series of modest structures that facilitate the museum and break the order of the original buildings, thus activating the site and adding a twenty-first century layer of construction to the complex.

These new buildings are in deliberate counterpoint to the original symmetrical structures. The language of the new elements is as strong and robust as the original colliery, but contrasts strongly with the decaying walls and crumbling masonry. The interior spaces, which are necessarily enclosed with carefully controlled natural and artificial light, slide between, through and around the original building.

Right:
The exterior
The retained elements are juxtaposed against the new building.

Far right:
View into the public space
The arches of the old building frame the courtyard.

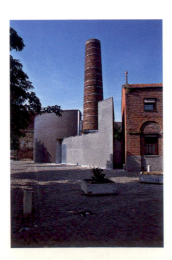

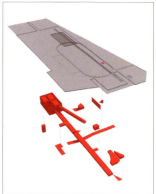

Above:
New and old
An exploded axonometric shows the order of the existing and the disorder of the new.

Left:
Threshold
The new gallery is asymmetrically off-set against the simple geometry of the existing building.

Above:
Free space
The open wall between
the exterior of the old building
and the gallery.

Right:
The Gipsoteca
The original plaster cast gallery
has classical order.

'The architecture of Carlo Scarpa is an authentic, powerful and coherent body of work. During the course of its production he dedicated himself to a lifetime of research into the balance between form and material; craft and tradition, memory and sensuality.'

George Ranalli

Balance

Name:
Plaster Cast Gallery,
The Canova Museum

Location:
Possagno, Italy

Date:
1957

Designer:
Carlo Scarpa

Interiors that are balanced do not need to be identical or even symmetrical; balance can be achieved through the careful positioning of objects, spaces or forms.

Carlo Scarpa was asked to design the extension to the original Canova Museum to celebrate the bicentenary of the artist's birth. The gallery (or gipsoteca), was a large, complete and composed classical building, Scarpa's extension is a modernist counterpoint to this monumentality. It is triangular in plan and appears to slide effortlessly through the space next to the gipsoteca.

The initial space of Scarpa's insertion is white, top lit and more or less cubic in shape. It has been slipped from the axis of the original foyer and thus encourages both visual and physical movement. The visitor follows their eyes around the corner and immediately appreciates the manner in which the space slides through the triangular room and into the courtyard beyond. The new and the old are separated by a lightwell that throws filtered natural light into the new gallery, reinforcing the sense of movement. The new and the old are different both in shape and in nature, but the classical and the modernist parts are similar in ambition and strength and are therefore balanced.

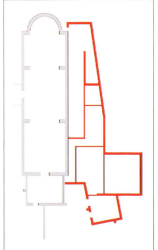

Above right:
View from the courtyard
Light and space flows through the gallery.

Right:
Plan
The drawing shows the ordered original building balanced with Scarpa's insertion.

Introduction > **Closed room** > Free plan

Rhythm

Name:
Post Office Savings Bank

Location:
Vienna, Austria

Date:
1904

Designer:
Otto Wagner

A rhythm of repeated elements can create order and control within an interior. These may be objects, structural elements or even spaces. Elements may then be placed within the space that conform to this rhythm or contrast with it. A dissimilar object placed within a series of similar ones will stand out, equally an element positioned at an angle will be revealed within an orthogonal organisation.

This post office in Vienna, Austria is widely regarded as one of the most important examples of early modern architecture: the structure and the cladding are quite clearly expressed, the bolts that hold the marble sheets in place are openly visible. The centrally placed main banking hall is a magnificent space, with exposed columns and a curved glass roof. A strong and controlling grid dictates the position of all the major elements within the space, from the aluminium hot air blowers to the glazed panels in the floor. The pattern or rhythm of this restraining grid organises the interior, thus liberating the in-between spaces for the post office customers.

Above:
The banking hall
The space is ordered by the grid.

Methods of organising space

'The top-lit banking hall was the closest
Wagner came to his ideal of a new
style derived from engineering forms.
The beautifully integrated, riveted
steel structure, glazing, light fittings,
cylindrical heat inlets and glass block
floor, and total absence of ornament
make it a landmark in the development
of modern architecture.'

Richard Weston

Below:
Plan of the building
The banking hall is placed at the
heart of the post office.

Above:
The entrance hall
The aluminium air vents
create rhythm.

Above:
**The floor and heating
elements**
The grid is reinforced by the
careful placement of the vents.

Above:
The glass floor
The glass floor emphasises
the rhythm of the grid.

Playstation

Name:
Mobile Home Voor Het
Kröller-Müller

Location:
Kröller-Müller Museum,
the Netherlands

Date:
1995

Designer:
Atelier Van Lieshout (AVL)

'…his caravans and campers do not merely express a utopian optimism, they display a desire for autonomy that is much more primitive, alluding to the vogue of survivalism, with all of its fascistic overtones. Above all, the sculptures, tools, pieces of furniture and built structures that Van Lieshout makes are direct and impulsive manifestations of a desire to create extensions of his own body.'
Bart Lootsma

A particular approach that has become more prevalent within all aspects of design is similar to the organisational technique used in playstation or computer games. A collection of events or objects are arranged in series, each is a complete entity and has to be fully appreciated before the viewer or competitor can move on. Just as the computer game player has to complete a particular level before they can enter the next experience. There is no interaction or movement between levels, although there is a theme that unites them. Interior designers can use this technique to create a series of different experiences or spaces.

Mobile Home by Atelier Van Lieshout is a deformed temporary structure that has been distorted to express the different activities that happen within the home. Each function is expressed as a grossly distorted protuberance that clings to the wall of the original structure. Each is recognisably complete and a total experience in its own right.

Above:
The enigmatic object
The functions spill from
the caravan.

Facing page, above:
The caravan in the landscape
The materials reflect the
individual function of the spaces.

Facing page, below:
**A series of temporary
habitable spaces**
The character of each
is expressed by its functional
autonomy.

Above:
The theatre set
The exaggerated perspective
of the fixed stage.

Methods of organising space

'This permanent setting, representing a city in the Renaissance style, only allowed for the performance of classical plays.'

Rob Krier

Addition

Name:
Teatro Olimpico

Location:
Vicenza, Italy

Date:
1580

Designer:
Andrea Palladio

Perfect interior spaces can be created within existing buildings to regularise an irregular space, and create order and generate formality. The designer may wish to take the approach of creating a completely new interior, which has little connection or relevance to the original space – a contained and internally focussed room.

The Teatro Olimpico is based on the ancient Roman principle of a fixed and elaborate architectural backdrop or proscenium with a stage in front of it.

It is a fixed and permanent autonomous element within an irregularly shaped building. This self-contained geometrical space contains the seating, the stage and the scenery, all of which are integrated with each other. The audience sit within the highly decorated half amphitheatre, which is terminated at the top layer by a colonnade of free-standing and attached columns. Statues of the gods stand upon the columns joining the audience in their appreciation of the performance.

The stage contains a permanently fixed street scene; seven streets recede away from the viewer with exaggerated perspective. This is created by narrowing the space between the walls and gradually raising the floor. The *trompe l'oeil* clouds painted onto the flat ceiling reinforce this exterior quality. Palladio has created a vision of classical theatre within the tight confines of a city context.

Above:
The classical street scene
The view through an opening in the Proscenium Screen.

The liberation of the internal walls from the structure allows for vast, open, free space. This section will explore the opportunities that this type of approach can offer.

Above:
The upper level of the gallery
The grid of the ceiling is visible suspended over the free space.

Right:
The exterior
The careful placement of the columns allows clear views between them.

Below right:
The upper level of the gallery
The upper level is in the centre, raised up on the podium.

Symmetry

Name:
New National Gallery

Location:
Berlin, Germany

Date:
1968

Designer:
Ludwig Mies van der Rohe

The structural revolution that led to the Free Plan was taken to the absolute extreme with the design of the New National Gallery, in Berlin, Germany. The building was conceived as a piece of steel and glass, modernist art placed upon a plinth. The exterior walls are completely glazed, immense columns support a massive overhanging roof, the corners are free and thus the interior space not only appears to be empty, but also recedes far beyond the limits of the building. Each elevation is treated identically, regardless of view or orientation, with just two well-proportioned black steel columns, which carry the huge flat plane of the roof. The arrangement on the interior is even more austere, although the structural grid is exposed within the ceiling, the space is free of structure and is therefore liberated. This allows the organisation of the temporary exhibitions space to be completely open and unrestricted.

Above:
View from the podium
The exterior clearly shows
the minimal grid and free plan
of the building.

Ludwig Mies van der Rohe
Ludwig Mies van der Rohe is regarded
as one of the pioneers of modern
architecture. He developed a method
of using an exposed steel structure
with plate glass infills to create rigorous
yet elegant spaces. Other significant
buildings include the Seagram Building
in New York (1958) and the German
Pavilion at the Barcelona Exhibition
of 1929, for which he also created
the celebrated Barcelona Chair. He is
famous for the motto: 'Less is More'.

Closed room > **Free plan**

Asymmetry

Name:
Kunsthal

Location:
Rotterdam, the Netherlands

Date:
1992

Designer:
Rem Koolhaas/OMA

Spaces that have been liberated from the constraints of load-bearing walls do not have to adhere to any fixed pattern or order. The walls, spaces and activities do not have to be placed in relation to the structure, they can be positioned in the location that is most suitable for the facilitation of the function.

The Kunsthal in Rotterdam, a museum for exhibitions and performances, is a compact building that contains a large exhibition space, distributed over three halls and two galleries. The building is situated on top of a small road and next to a 15-foot-high dyke. A series of massive ramps and roads carve through the art gallery space, creating the sense that the city is pouring through the structure. The concept is of a mobius strip-like building, a promenade that loops around and through the inclined auditorium, through a side gallery and up on to the roof. This results in a confusion or complexity to the nature and function of the spaces, an asymmetrical interior is created.

Top:
The open auditorium
The circulation flows through the lecture hall.

Above:
Circulation
The free plan allows visual links to exist through transparent walls.

'The building was conceived as a square crossed by two routes…With these givens, and the fact that these crossings would divide the square into four parts, the challenge became; how to design a museum as four autonomous projects – a sequence of contradictory experiences which would nevertheless form a continuous spiral. In other words how to imagine a spiral in four separate squares.'

Rem Koolhaas

Above:
The layers of the building
Axonometric diagram showing the architectural promenade.

Left:
The split levels of the folding slab floors
The ramps and stairs of the circulation are threaded between the columns.

Above:
The interior
The planes of box-jointed marble define and organise the space.

Right:
Free space
View from the pool towards the main function room.

Balance

Name:
Barcelona Pavilion

Location:
Barcelona, Spain

Date:
1929

Designer:
Ludwig Mies van der Rohe

A building or space can be organised to give a sense of balance, evenness and strength while still possessing qualities of transience and movement.

The Barcelona Pavilion was a temporary structure, built as the German Pavilion for the 1929 International Exhibition. It was designed to project an image of an international, open and modern German state. The building is composed of sliding vertical and horizontal planes, tied together by the tight formation of eight columns. The single-storey structure has a flat plane roof supported by elegant cruciform-shaped, chrome-covered, steel columns. Two rectangular pools, one at either end, tie the building together. The smaller pool is placed centrally to the structure and is surrounded by high walls, while the larger is off-centre and is free. Between these two are a series of barely defined spaces that slip into each other. Mies van der Rohe used a simple, but expensive palette of materials: marble and onyx walls, tinted reflective glass, stainless steel and travertine. The composition is not symmetrical, but it is balanced. There is a sense of perpetual movement within the intense rhythm of spaces and planes.

'The new architecture has broken through the wall, thus destroying the separateness of inside and outside. Walls are no longer load bearing: they have been reduced to points of support. This gives rise to a new, open plan, totally different from the classical one, in that interior and exterior space interpenetrate.'

Theo van Doesburg

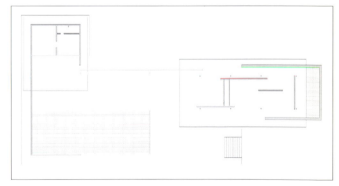

Top:
The exterior of the pavilion
The roof appears to float over the minimal structure.

Above:
Plan of the pavilion
The drawing shows the balance between the open and closed, the bright and dark spaces.

Closed room > Free plan

Right:
Site plan
The plan shows the orthogonal rhythmn of the gallery in contrast with the more organic nature of the public spaces.

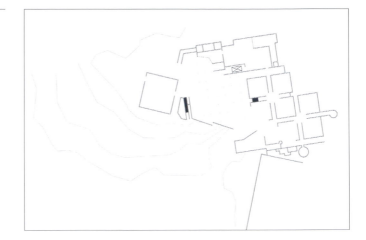

Rhythm

Name:
Municipal Museum

Location:
Mönchengladbach, Germany

Date:
1972–1981

Designer:
Hans Hollein

Spaces that are enclosed and contained can still possess rhythm. A repeated series of identical rooms can project stability, but if the order and sequence can be observed, then rhythm is also apparent. Axial views are especially good at demonstrating movement, repetition and order; all of which contribute to the rhythm of an interior.

The Municipal Museum in Mönchengladbach is a building that responds to its context, the strong orthogonal galleries are a direct reference to the urban grain of the city, while the more organic free flowing public spaces suggest the countryside. In contrast to the standard large museums being constructed at the time, as exemplified by the Pompidou Centre of 1977, Hollein designed different types of spaces for the different museum functions, each reflecting the activity that occurred within.

The solid and substantial gallery spaces are square and are accessed on the diagonal; the room are entered at the corners. This very modernist attitude of expressing a lack of structure at the corner is also a very sensible approach to gallery design, as corner spaces are very difficult to display art in. This emphasis on the diagonal is reinforced by the saw-toothed roofs, which are placed diagonally over the spaces. This rhythm of square contained rooms controls and organises the north and west sides of the building, but it does not overpower the more liberated arrangement to the south. The series of identical enclosed galleries provides the neutral background for the display of art.

'I have always considered architecture as an art. To me architecture is not primarily the solution of a problem, but the making of a statement. Within the two poles of architectural activity, architecture as ritual, and architecture as a means of preservation of body-temperature, my search is for the absolute, as well as for the needs and constraints, which also generate form.'

Hans Hollein

Top:
Threshold
The visual link between gallery spaces.

Above:
Axis
The galleries are a progression of spaces arranged on the diagonal.

Left:
The gallery rising out of the landscape
The rythmn of the roof above the galleries is clearly visible from the outside.

Playstation

Name:
Dutch Pavilion, Expo2000

Location:
Hanover, Germany

Date:
2000

Designer:
MVRDV

Buildings or spaces can be arranged so that they have little or no connection with what went before or will go after. The designer can construct a narrative of a series of unrelated but themed experiences, each self-contained, and often with distinct starting and finishing points. This is not unlike a playstation or computer game. Each level must be completed before the player can move on; there is no visual link between the levels and little psychological connection.

The Dutch Pavilion is a fine example of the playstation building; it was conceived as a reminder of land saved from the sea. It is literally six stacked floors of Dutch landscape. The visitor takes the lift to the top floor, and then gradually makes their way down, beginning with the windmills on the roof. The size of each level is the same: exactly 1,000 square meters, but each treated differently; the fourth floor contains a forest and is supported with tree trunks. The fifth has lecture theatres and the ground floor contains a grotto. The many different aspects of Dutch life are presented together in a highly efficient, space saving structure.

Above:
The stacked pavilion
The different activities on each level are clearly visible from the exterior of the building.

Right:
The third floor caves
The enlarged structures grow up from the floor and down from the ceiling.

'MVRDV displays the maximum spatial implications of each layer in a 'data-scape', an updated version of what was formerly called a design situation and planning envelope, which clarifies the optimal solutions.'

Baart Lootsma

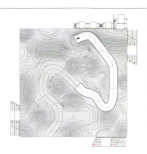

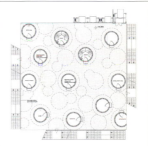

Above:
Interior Dutch landscape
The first floor is a field of flowers.

Top to bottom right:

Plan
Third floor.

Plan
First floor.

Plan
Ground floor.

Section
This drawing shows how each floor is occupied with a different activity.

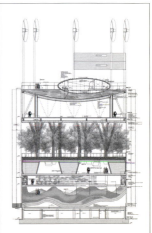

Closed room > **Free plan**

'What is most striking about today's architecture is the impurity, the permissive joining together of the logical and the illogical, the structural and the unstructured, functional and non-functional elements.'

Juhani Pallasma

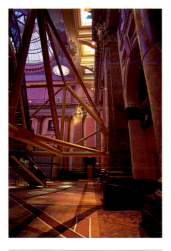

Above:
Detail of the structure
The new theatre is suspended from the columns of the original building.

Facing page:
The theatre in context
The hall comfortably accommodates the theatre.

Addition

Name:
Royal Exchange Theatre

Location:
Manchester, UK

Date:
1977

Designer:
Levitt Bernstein Associates

A new or alien element can be placed within a measured and balanced room or space to create an atmosphere that is no longer balanced, but one that encourages both visual and physical movement. If the object is situated off-centre, if it is misaligned, then emphasis can be placed upon one space and removed from another.

The Royal Exchange Theatre in Manchester was inserted into the central hall of the old exchange building. The original space was huge and strong, with three glass domes supported by gigantic columns. The new theatre really does appear as an alien element within these surroundings. It was constructed at the same time as the Pompidou Centre and shares that optimistic, high-tech, space age style. Massive trusses take the weight of the theatre and these in turn transfer the weight on to huge columns, thus allowing the space-ship theatre to float within the space. The theatre is very self-contained, it is by necessity focussed internally, but its placement off-centre means that physical and visual movement within the hall is encouraged. The resultant larger space is used for the foyer activities, such as a café and bar, while the smaller is used primarily for circulation. It is an additive element that activates and invigorates the empty building. The empty space of the foyer is balanced by the energy of the theatre.

The existing building can be regarded as a guidebook containing much of the information necessary to provide the impetus for redesign. We can call interiors of this kind 'responsive'. This reading of the original space can present certain clues or pointers for the nature and character of the redesign. Not just the significant question of structural stability, but also for such issues as rhythm, movement and space. This process can be as destructive as it is constructive. The designer or architect may strip away or remove elements in order to reveal the hidden meaning of the building, before adding elements that interpret this analysis and form the basis of the redesign. The form of the existing influences the form of the new: form follows form.

Responsive interiors can be catalogued into three sections: Intervened, Inserted and Installed. The architect or designer will use one of these methods to form the basis of a redesign: intervened interiors will thoroughly alter the existing building; inserted interiors will make use of the placement of an independent object, the nature of which is governed by the original building, and installed interiors will house an arrangement of a series of elements within a space that are closely related to it but will not alter it.

Name:
Town Hall

Location:
Utrecht, The Netherlands

Date:
1999

Designer:
EMBT (Enric Miralles–Benedetta Tagliabue)

Methods of organising space > **Responsive interiors** > Autonomous interiors

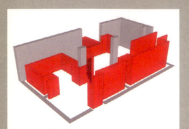

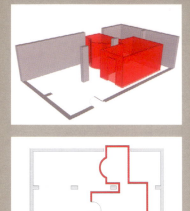

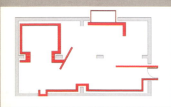

Intervened interiors

Intervened interiors are created when the architect or designer reveals the qualities of the existing building and translates these into the new design. The reading of the building will lead the architect or designer to recognise the character of the original and use this as the impetus for the remodelling. This uncovering of the qualities of the original can be very intrusive and sometimes involves extensive demolition as well as construction. The interventions can alter or change the existing building so much that it can no longer viably exist independently, the new and the old can become irretrievably combined. This process is frequently exploited by the designers of museums, who strive to simultaneously exhibit both the building and its contents.

Inserted interiors

Inserted interiors establish a very close relationship between the existing building and the new interior. The architect or designer will design a single striking element to be inserted into the existing space. This distinct component may contain a number of different functional and servicing activities that can easily be separated from the main activity of the building. These could include circulation, private meeting rooms or even huge autonomous activities such as lecture theatres. The designer may exploit the structural integrity of the existing building to support the new interior or may use the exact dimensions of a particular space to dictate the exact dimensions of the new inserted element. This technique is particularly effective when the language of the new element is at odds with the existing building: for the contemporary insertion to be dynamically juxtaposed against the crumbling ruins of the ancient building.

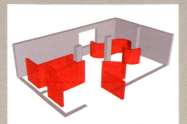

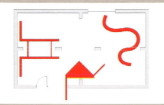

Left to right:

Three-dimensional drawing
of an intervened interior.

Three-dimensional drawing
of an inserted interior.

Three-dimensional drawing
of an installed interior.

Left to right:

Plan of an intervened interior.

Plan of an inserted interior.

Plan of an installed interior.

Installed interiors

Installed interiors allow the existing
building and the elements of the redesign
to exist independently. The old influences
the design of the new, the arrangement
and placement of the installed elements
are dictated by the form of the existing,
but they do not alter the structure or size
of the original space – they simply react
to it. Installation artists, when creating
a response to a given space, will often use
this technique; it is commonly employed
by exhibition designers and is especially
appropriate when dealing with historic
or listed buildings. The artist, designer or
architect may, for example, use the
rhythm of the window openings or
structural columns to measure the
pattern of the new interior.

The interiors in this category draw their character directly from the qualities of the existing building. An intervened interior can alter or change the existing building irrevocably so that the new and the old no longer exist independently.

Name:
Castelvecchio Museum

Location:
Verona, Italy

Date:
1957–64

Designer:
Carlo Scarpa

Intervention is a response that will use the qualities of the original building to inform the design of the new elements. Carlo Scarpa was the architect responsible for the restoration and remodelling of the Castelvecchio Museum in Verona, Italy. By the use of creative demolition he uncovered the various historic strata of the building. The castle was a complicated confusion of many eras of construction and Scarpa strove to explore and isolate the various phases of building to reveal the complex and rich beauty of the place.

A series of carefully designed interventions were strategically placed within the building. The dynamic quality of the modernist elements contrasted with the classical, static nature of the existing building. These elements were designed to both support and highlight the exhibits and also to control the thresholds and movement through the building. The sparingly positioned elements encourage the visitor to move from one artefact to the next, to turn around, to move into or out of the direct light or shadow, to circulate in a composed and slightly unselfconscious manner while appreciating the works of art and the quality and character of the castle.

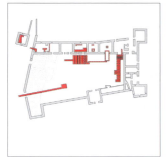

Above:
View of the exterior
A representation of the interior can be seen projecting out of an opening at ground level and as a recessed screen at first floor level.

Above right:
Statue of Cangrande
The pivotal point between the city walls and the castle is scraped away to reveal a backdrop for the Cangrande Statue.

Right:
Plan of Castelvecchio
The clear and ordered organisation of the original building provided a counterpoint for Scarpa's intervention.

Carlo Scarpa

Carlo Scarpa's approach was to take all the cues for the remodelling from the existing building, with a particular attention to scale, light, form and movement, so his design approach was one of part archaeology, part analysis and part new construction. Most of his work was carried out in northern Italy but his masterpiece was the remodelling of the Castelvecchio.

Above:
View of Castelvecchio interior
The central axis links the interior spaces to the central monument of the Cangrande statue.

Introduction > Intervened > Inserted

Intervened: Focus study 2

Name:
Küppersmühle Museum of
Modern Art, Grothe Collection

Location:
Duisburg, Germany

Date:
1999

Designer:
Herzog & de Meuron

An intervention can heighten
the basic character of an
existing building. The old brick
warehouse in the dock area
of Duisburg that was to be
converted into the Küppersmühle
Museum of Modern Art, had
a massive monumental quality.
The proportions were almost
classical; the main façade was
a simple rhythm of recessed
windows set against brick
supports all of which sat upon
a large uncomplicated plinth.
The scale was huge and
the architects Herzog & de
Meuron reinforced this with an
intervention to this main façade.

By recognising the position
of the new galleries they were
able to control the manner in
which light entered the building
and began by blocking the
windows to render the façade
blank. A series of window
openings were then punched
into the façade in a contemporary
and audacious manner, with
little regard for the internal
organisation of the building.
This reinforced the monumental
quality of the building while
accommodating the spaces
of the new galleries.

'Architecture is bound to situation. Unlike music,
painting, sculpture, film and literature, a construction
(non mobile) is intertwined with the experience
of place.'

Steven Holl

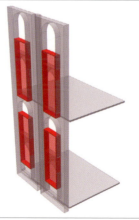

Above:
**View of Küppersmühle
gallery interior**
The new windows are placed
on the very edge of the building,
thus accentuating the depth
of the wall.

Left:
Gallery façade
The incisions are a recognition
of the new interior function.

Right:
Küppersmühle façade
The monumental quality
of the building is disrupted
by the new incisions.

Above:
View of the church interior
The circulation insulates the chapel from the outside world.

Right:
View of the worshipping space
The triple height chapel is illuminated by concealed lighting.

Intervened: Focus study 3

Name:
Fourth Church of Christ Scientist

Location:
Manchester, UK

Date:
1998

Designer:
OMI Architects

The complex process of adapting buildings for new uses can sometimes contain a destructive element. The building may have to undergo extensive demolition before the constructive process of remodelling can begin. This is the approach that OMI used when they carved a chapel from the innermost spaces of a disused office block. Their careful analysis focussed primarily inwards, upon the quality of the individual spaces, the relationship between one room and another and of each floor with the one below or above. The positions of the doors, the windows and the circulation areas all contributed to this intricate composition.

The chapel itself is an atmospheric triple-height space cocooned within the depths of the building. It is subtly lit from large west-facing windows and the long evening sun glows through the circulation areas to provide the congregation with secondary yet evocative light. This is reinforced by artificial light secreted behind structural openings, and thus the chapel is radiant with hidden luminosity. A tiny reading room was inserted into the barely double-height space of the reception area and bookshop. This clever little structure contains bookshelves and a service desk at the lower level and a quiet retreat above.

The reading of the interior spaces of the original building provided the catalyst for the organisation of the remodelling. The whole structure is a carefully composed series of delicate and subtle details, each exposing the qualities of the existing context while also enhancing the new function.

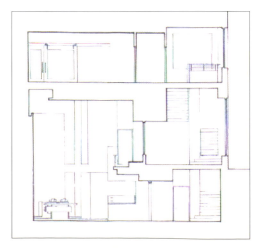

Left:
Section through the church
The compact interior is a collection of intricate spaces.

The interiors in this category establish a very close relationship between the existing building and the new interior. The new element is built to an exact fit of the existing building.

Inserted: Focus study 1

Name:
Documentation Centre for
the Third Reich, Nazi Party
Rally Grounds

Location:
Nuremberg, Germany

Date:
2002

Designer:
Günther Domenig

A contemporary insertion can act as a symbolic and forceful statement. The kongresshalle in Nuremberg was the centrepiece of the 'City of Congress'; it was planned by Albert Speer to host the great Nazi rallies of the 1930s. The huge building was vacant from 1945, mainly because nobody knew what to do with it, and equally, nobody wanted to simply raze it. The architect Günther Domenig won the competition to remodel the great building in 1998. The approach he took was to diagonally pierce the structure, directly against the grain of the building, with an uncompromising and dynamic element. This aggressively sharp shaft of glass and steel serves as a circulation route through the building, linking the entrance with the massive courtyard at the back of the building. The brutality with which it cuts the existing spaces is left exposed; the raw and scarred walls are not repaired. The insertion is an unambiguous and powerful statement of repentance and remembering.

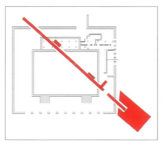

Top:
Entrance shard
The shard of circulation explodes from the building.

Above:
Section through the building
Diagonal cross section through the courtyard block.

Right:
Plan of kongresshalle
The plan shows exactly how violent the insertion is.

'…a conversion only succeeds when there is a good match between new function and existing form.'

Philippe Robert

Left:
Kongresshalle entrance
The entrance is placed on a diagonal axis through the kongresshalle.

Below:
Interior route
The circulation bridge hovers over the courtyard before penetrating through the masonry structure.

Intervened > Inserted > Installed

Inserted: Focus study 2

Name:
The Archbishopric Museum

Location:
Hamar, Norway

Date:
1967–79

Designer:
Sverre Fehn

An insertion does not need to be an efficient, compact structure; it can be a free-ranging and abundant construction. In his remodelling of the Archbishopric Museum, Sverre Fehn created an awkward, loose circulation route threading through the ruins of a medieval fortress that explains and reveals the history and beauty of the place it navigates.

The museum is a collection of long thin buildings gathered around an open courtyard and the new path is a huge fluctuating structure that controls the route taken by the visitor, while also revealing the quality of the ancient building.

This brutal concrete element begins as a ramp in the courtyard and then swings away from the building before performing a u-turn and diving through an opening at the junction between the south and central wings. Once inside, it acts as a bridge, navigating the route through what were once the main rooms of the settlement. Huge floating boxes of shuttered concrete are attached to the bridge and these hold the precious archaeological discoveries belonging to the museum. The language of the new insertion is uncompromising, but it is balanced by the equally hard nature of the original building; unfinished concrete against stone and rubble. The walkway slides exactly through the existing openings and takes advantage of the light from the original windows and doors.

Above:
Courtyard ramp
The uncompromisingly brutal ramp begins its journey in the courtyard.

Right:
Diagram of the museum
The awkward circulation route threads through the enigmatic buildings.

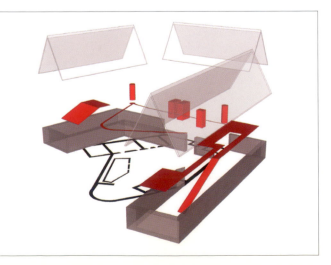

Above:
Bridge through the interior
The walkway is suspended above the archeological remains in the main hall.

Left:
Concrete box
The imposing shuttered concrete box is attached to the bridge and holds the precious archeological finds.

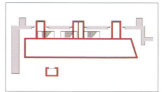

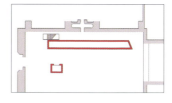

Inserted: Focus study 3

Name:
Marienkirche and Library

Location:
Muncheberg, Germany

Date:
1994

Designer:
Klaus Block

An insertion can act to separate one particular activity from another. This is the approach that Klaus Block took when he remodelled the Marienkirche in Muncheberg. The insertion was used to isolate the specific types of function. The church had been derelict for half a century and as a consequence, when the time came to rebuild and remodel it, the parish was insufficiently large to support the whole building. A secular and spiritual partnership was formed; half of the building would belong to the church and the other half would form the local library. The library elements were collected into a sculptural four-storey freestanding element; a tall, graceful steel-framed vessel that was built into the nave, thus leaving the chancel free for worship.

The timber-clad structure rises from the floor in an elegant curve; it is smaller at ground level to give a greater area for circulation within the church and it then bows out to create larger library rooms at the upper levels. The library is connected to the sidewall of the church by an open staircase; this ties the two together and also assimilates any discrepancies between the clean, exact steel and glass structure and the crumbling stonework. The body of the library is glazed and then clad with ash louvres to give the structure a semi-transparent quality, while also providing privacy and separation. The rhythm of the slats changes to respond to the activities within the rooms they enclose. The architect has in this way created a dynamic and moving relationship between the powerful structure of the original building and the simple form of the insertion.

Above:
Plans of the church
The library is smaller at ground level but swells to accommodate a meeting room on the top floor.

Young People's Museum, Berlin
Klaus Block took a similar approach to the design of the Young People's Museum in Berlin. A large structure, similar to a climbing frame, containing different types and shapes of child-sized spaces was placed in the centre of the century-old Elijah Church in Berlin.

Responsive interiors

Above right:
Library 'box'
The timber cladding reflects
the nature of the very different
activities within the building.

Right:
The library stairs
The staircase is placed between
the library and the walls of the
original building and assimilate
any discrepancies between
the two.

The interiors in this category allow the existing building and the new elements of the design to exist independently of one another.

Installed: Focus study 1

Name:
Glenlyon Church

Location:
Victoria, Australia

Date:
2004

Designer:
Multiplicity

Restrictions on a listed building may mean that it can only be altered in a limited manner. The architect or designer may respond to this challenge by carefully placing new, seemingly ephemeral elements within the place so that they do not touch or alter the building – they only respond to it. This approach was taken by Multiplicity when they converted the Glenlyon Church into a family home.

The designers began by making a detailed study of the building; this initially involved measuring, surveying and even drawing every individual stone within the building's envelope.

'It's a form of madness. But our practice spends a great deal of time just measuring and getting a sense of the space.'[1]

Within the capacious hall of the church, Multiplicity installed a large open architectural structure made from steel, acrylic, glass and timber. The vivid construction responds to the shape and rhythm of the existing building in a quite distinct and contrasting language, although the orthogonal nature of the new element is as robust as the original building.

This bright green structure further divides the space within the church. The smaller area next to the front door is for reclining and receiving guests, while the area on the other side is the dining room and kitchen. The bedrooms, bathrooms, study, storage and services are all gathered together in the complex three-dimensional installation. The study is situated on the upper level and hangs over the dining and kitchen area, much like a modern pulpit.

The building has not lost its ecclesiastical character; the exterior has a distinctly gothic revival style, much of it remaining unaltered. Indeed, even some of the stained glass has been retained. The interior walls have been stripped and painted white to emphasise the exposed roof trusses. The new elements do not touch the old building yet they are derived from its scale and proportions, juxtaposing the new against the old.

'We wanted to create texture and relief, something that evokes the past in an abstracted way.'[2]

1
O'Sullivan, T. 2005. *Indesign*, vol. 20 (February 2005), pp.138–145

2
Sioux Clark, ibid

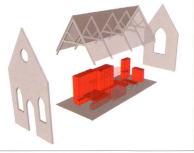

Opposite page:
View of the church exterior
The exterior of the building
remains relatively unchanged.

Top left:
View of the lounge
The lounge slides from
underneath the master bedroom.

Above:
**View of the dining and
living space**
The autonomous structure
sits enigmatically within the
cavernous church hall.

Left:
Kitchen in the altar
The free-standing kitchen
occupies the former altar space
of the church.

Top:
Diagram of the interior
The new insertion is merely
contained within the walls
of the church.

Installed: Focus study 2

Name:
Pheasant Barn

Location:
Faversham, UK

Date:
2000

Designer:
Circus Architects

'The combination of old structures and new uses calls for specific solutions depending upon the relevant object and task…the genius loci is reinvigorated through conversion.'

Johan Jessen and Jochem Schneider

An installed interior will acknowledge the qualities of the existing building without actually altering them. This approach is especially suitable for work within listed buildings as substantial or irreversible changes to the building are unlikely to be permitted.

This was the problem that Circus Architects faced when they were asked to convert a Grade II listed, seventeenth-century barn into a family house. They were unable to change the exterior of the building or touch four large, exposed timber trusses that supported the wooden weather-boarded barn. This led the architects to design elements that just slipped between the existing structure, allowing the new and the old existing simultaneously without intruding upon each other.

The four trusses effectively divided the interior into five sections. Accordingly, within this rhythm, two floating balconies were installed, leaving the ground floor area free for family activities, while providing bedroom privacy in the floating structures. The undersides of the mezzanines also provided some order to the lower level by dictating the position of particular activities.

Above:
The floating bedroom
The language of the new and old is radically different.

Responsive interiors

Top:
View through the barn interior, towards the floating bedroom
The old is not compromised by the new.

Above left:
House axonometric
The rhythm of the existing counterpoints the disorder of the installation.

Above right:
Section through the barn
The ordered timber structure contrasts with the new, dynamic, pure white elements.

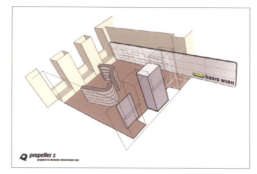

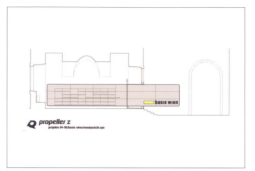

Installed: Focus study 3

Name:
Basis Wien, Information Centre
for Contemporary Art

Location:
Vienna, Austria

Date:
1997

Designer:
propeller z

An installed object can evoke
feelings of lightness and
movement when placed within
a calm and measured space.
Designers, propeller z, juxtaposed
a long interactive screen against
the calm interior of a single
room in their remodelling of an
eighteenth-century block in the
museum quarter of Vienna.

This elongated element is lit
from behind and below and
appears to float. The function
of the long silver plane changes
as it travels through the coffered
room. It is used for the storage
of archive material, for small
exhibition display and to
accommodate computer and
other communication equipment
within the public area. It then
glides out through a new
transparent glass door set into
the Baroque façade and signals
the entrance to the centre with
a simple yellow logo. The screen
is constructed in a most simple
manner; cut sheets of aluminium
are attached to a straightforward
steel frame using kitchen cabinet
fittings. The lack of polish within
the construction is balanced
by the decaying qualities of the
original room. The impact of this
long aluminium element is huge,
but the damage to the original
vaulted space is minimal.

Top left:
**Axonometric diagram
of the project**
The screen is part of a family
of installed elements.

Top right:
Section through the interior
The screen is an independent
element that links the outside
with the inside.

Above:
Interior wall
The backlit screen appears
to float within the interior space.

propeller z
Designers, propeller z, have developed a game, 'super trumpf' (not unlike Top Trumps) involving the work of their practice. It has categories such as floor area, construction time and budget. The exhibition building; Meteorit, had the longest thinking time at 11,532 hours, while the portable sound reproduction unit, Spin Off, had the shortest at just 13 hours.

Left:
View of the entrance
The screen slides through the entrance to advertise the information centre.

The shaping or organisation of interior space can sometimes be regarded as an independent process, constrained only by the extent of the established spatial volume. The original building can be thought of as an envelope that contains the new interior while exerting very little influence upon it. The new elements are positioned within the space, making reference only to themselves, not to the container that they are placed within. This approach can be used to standardise unusual spaces or structural systems, thus creating what appears to be a composed and ordered space from what is actually irregular and unbalanced. Considerations such as function, style, fashion, surface treatment and contemporary art and design can be discussed through the arrangement and juxtaposition of form and lighting.

Autonomous interiors can be catalogued into three sections: Disguised, Assembled and Combined. The architect or designer will use the disguised approach to line or hide the existing space, the assembled system to fill the space with new objects and when these two are used simultaneously, the method can be described as combined.

Name:
'Semi-detached', Duveen Hall

Location:
Tate Britain, London, UK

Date:
2004

Designer:
Michael Landy

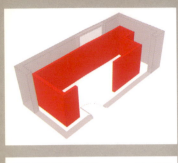

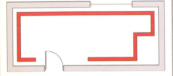

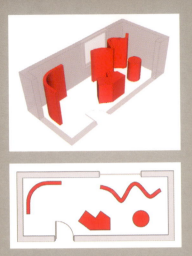

Disguised interiors

Disguised interiors treat the existing interior as a shell that is to be hidden or camouflaged. The architect or designer will create a new lining to cover the surfaces of the original space. This will, in effect, give the appearance of a completely new interior. It can provide an irregular space with balance and a sense of proportion that it would not naturally have. This lining or veil has qualities that are independent of the original building; its material, structural and physical characteristics are very much self-governing; dictated by function, style or whim. It is constrained only by the size of the space that it inhabits. The lining will usually barely touch the building's walls at all. This screen can be used to conceal unsightly or intrusive elements, service activities such as circulation or bathrooms can be secreted behind it and it can even fold to hide away whole rooms. This approach is typically used within retail design.

Assembled interiors

Assembled interiors are generally anonymous spaces that do little more than contain a series of usually interconnected objects. The space itself is typically undistinguished and is, as a rule, treated in a neutral manner. The idea is for attention to be drawn away from the qualities of the building and for the focus to be upon the elements displayed within the space. This is typically the approach that an exhibition designer would take: the collection of exhibits, all of which relate to each other, are displayed in a fairly indistinct room. The objects interact with each other, the rhythm and placement of each is carefully planned with great consideration for those other related exhibits, and as such, the installation is designed to be independent from the form and structure of the existing space.

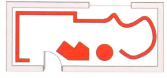

Left to right:

Three-dimensional drawing of a disguised interior.

Three-dimensional drawing of an assembled interior.

Three-dimensional drawing of a combined interior.

Left to right:

Plan of a disguised interior.

Plan of an assembled interior.

Plan of a combined interior.

Combined interiors

Combined interiors bring together the disguised and assembled approaches. The existing space is regarded as a neutral box that is lined or hidden. This newly formed space is then inhabited by a series or collection of elements, all interacting with each other and with the lining or screen, but not with the original space or building. The only constraint is size, which dictates exactly how much of this particular design concept can fit into the space. This approach is typical of most mainstream retail design. The designer will develop a concept that is transferable – nationally or even internationally. The shop walls are lined with display units, while the interior space contains freestanding cabinets or counters. The style will distinguish a particular brand and the design has to be sufficiently flexible to allow it to adapt to many different spaces and locations.

Introduction > Disguised

The interiors in this category treat the existing as a shell that is to be hidden or camouflaged. The interior will often consist of a new lining that disguises the surface of the existing space.

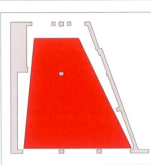

Disguised: Focus study 1

Title:
Oki-ni

Location:
London, UK

Date:
2001

Designer:
6a Architects

An uneven or crooked interior can be provided with order by the insertion of a facing or lining. This new element will have its own organisation and geometry and will inflict this discipline upon the existing space.

Oki-ni, which means 'thank you' in the Osaka dialect, occupies what used to be two adjoining retail spaces. This interior space was both irregular and slightly unknown because the architects were unable to survey the building before work commenced on site.

6a proposed a horizontal 'tray' that could be slid into the space, unifying both halves and absorbing the central structural column, which had been hidden in the separating partition wall. The tray was able to accommodate any irregularities in the outline of the space and thus created a meaningful order to the retail space. The structure of Russian oak controls and delineates the floor area and the upturn at the edges exhibits and displays the range of clothing and accessories. Clothes are hung from the exaggerated 'skirting' and are also draped over the large felt stacks in the centre of the space. The interstitial spaces behind the walls contain the subsidiary services such as storage, changing rooms and staff areas. The simple new element houses all of the shop's functional requirements while also inflicting rigor upon an uneven and unfortunate space.

Above left:
Diagram of the interior
The Russian oak 'tray' controls and disguises the space.

Top:
Concept model of the new lining
A simple model shows the designer's strategy of a new regular lining placed within an irregular space.

Above:
Plan of the interior
The plan view shows the difference between the new and the old.

Autonomous interiors

Above:
Interior of the space
The stack of felt sits enigmatically
in the space.

Left:
The interior from outside
The exaggerated skirting does not
reach the ceiling of the space.

Above:
The atmospheric interior
Upper level mirrors
exaggerate what is actually
a very intimate space.

Right:
The façade of the bar
A vivid representation of the
American flag advertises the bar.

Disguised: Focus study 2

Name:
American Bar/Karntner Bar

Location:
Vienna, Austria

Date:
1907

Designer:
Adolf Loos

An interior can be created to clad the existing interior envelope of the space it is to inhabit. It will completely cover over the internal walls, floor and ceiling. Adolf Loos explored the principles of cladding, whether of the interior or the exterior. He regarded covering as the oldest architectural detail, and that this mask should be truthful to the materials used.

The Karntner or American Bar uses skillful manipulation of a small space in Vienna. It is situated on a quiet side street, Karntner Durchgang and the outside signage is a representation of the American flag in gaudy-coloured glass, a provocative gesture in the city where Loos was renowned for his caustic character and controversial newspaper column, 'Das Andere'.

The inside is significantly different to the exterior: a skillful composition of marble, onyx, mirror and timber lines the space to form a discrete, intimate interior. The space is given careful order through the organisation of Skyros marble pillars and beams, reinforced by a veined marble coffered ceiling and then exaggerated by mirrors on the end walls, in effect 'multiplying the image to infinity'[1]. This creates endless rooms beyond the solidity of the timber lining and exaggerates the theatricality of the tiny room. The mahogany and leather furniture and brass counter are organised around the edges of the room, thus leaving the axial centre of the space for circulation. The modest space seats only 20 or so, and yet is not claustrophobic, thus ensuring an interior of both order and intimacy.

1
Gravagnuolo, B. and Rossi, A. 1982. *Adolf Loos*. New York: Edizioni.

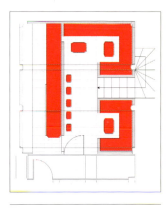

Above:
Interior plan
The plan reveals how tightly organised the interior is.

Raumplan
Adolf Loos (1870–1930) developed the notion of 'Raumplan' or space-plan, an intricate three-dimensional organisation of space. This is most perfectly realised in three houses: the Moller House, the Müller House and the Tristan Tzara House.

Above:
The chapel interior
The blue wall appears to float between the floor and the ceiling.

Right:
Site plan
The dual-space, one-room chapel is at the heart of the cemetery.

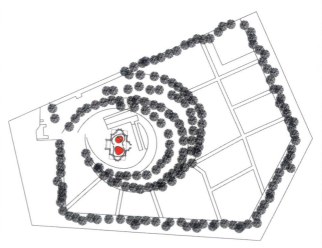

Disguised: Focus study 3

Name:
Chapel St Mary of the Angels

Location:
Rotterdam, the Netherlands

Date:
2001

Designer:
Mecanoo

A disguised approach can provide a contemporary interpretation of an old building. This attitude guided the enigmatic translation of the Chapel St Mary of the Angels by architects, Mecanoo.

The neo-classical chapel is situated at the centre of the St Lawrence cemetery, which was designed by H.J. van der Brink in 1865 and intended to resemble an Italian Campo Santo, a field of the dead. The chapel was troubled with subsidence and has been replaced twice.

The present chapel is constructed within the remains of the outer structural wall of the original building. Mecanoo placed a lightweight, blue screen that meanders within the confines of the ruined walls. It encircles both the congregation and the altar area to create an intimate dual-spaced, one-room chapel. The rectangular roof, constructed as a single curved plane, appears to float above this contained space. Natural light is admitted into the space through the glazed panels at the base and the top of the blue screens, thus giving the impression of weightlessness; the walls and the roof seem to be hovering. At night, artificial light glows through these windows, furthering the impression of movement and exaggerating the ephemeral qualities of the whole building.

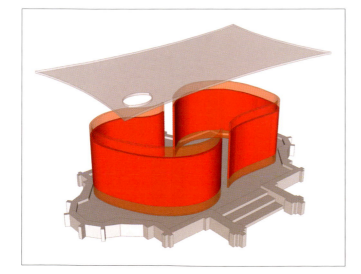

Above:
The view across the cemetery to the chapel
The chapel hovers above the cemetery.

Left:
Diagram of the chapel
The chapel is contained within the ruined walls of the original building.

The interiors in this category are defined by the character of the newly designed elements, rather than the neutral container in which they are placed. Their arrangement is designed to be independent from the form and structure of the existing space.

Assembled: Focus study 1

Name:
Studio and Residence

Location:
Omaha, USA

Date:
1999

Designer:
Randy Brown Architects

Assembled interiors are frequently anonymous spaces that contain independent structures. These are often enigmatic one-offs or sequential elements that enclose new functions yet do not make contact with the walls of the existing space.

In a non-descript 1970s school building in Omaha, Nebraska, Randy Brown has installed an autonomous object that is both a home for his wife and himself and an office for four designers. The elegant timber and steel structure is assembled using off-the-peg sections of material from the local hardware store. The DIY aesthetic lends itself to a temporary piece of furniture – a factor that helped Brown to persuade the local council that it was furniture rather than new-build and hence ease its transition though planning.

The three-dimensional structure has effectively split the building both vertically and horizontally: the first floor contains the private family bedroom and a roof terrace, while the ground floor is used for the more public activities; the studio, meeting room and the service areas. Vertical circulation, bookcases, the dining/meeting room and the sleeping loft are actually situated within the structure or 'container'. The Browns occupied the building during the remodelling, and the design of the container changed as it was being built: elements were moved around until a satisfactory relationship between all the different parts was reached. The anonymity of the building merely provides the space and shell for the new dynamic interior.

Top:
View towards the screen
A screen divides the conference/dining room from the reception.

Above:
View through the structure
The stair to the private area is placed discretely behind the structure.

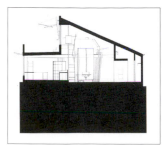

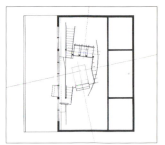

Above left:
Section through the interior
The central structure provides three-dimensional connections within the building.

Above centre and right:
Ground and first floor plans
The structure is situated centrally and divides the private and public areas.

Left:
Dining/meeting room
A collection of off-the-peg elements dictates the form of the structure.

Assembled: Focus study 2

Name:
Fendi Showroom

Location:
Paris, France

Date:
2002

Designer:
Lazzarini Pickering Studio

Lazzarini Pickering devised a geometric language for the flagship Fendi showroom in Paris. The concept, which characterises the opulent luxurious brand, is internationally transferable. The image is opulent, dynamic and generous; long sculptural elements of architectural proportions interact three-dimensionally with each other. The units towards the centre climb to form a three-dimensional sculptural staircase, emphasising the upper floors, while others slide delicately through the shop, exaggerating the length and space, thus ensuring that the entire shop is on view. The units that touch the edges of the space, (that is the floors and the walls) are of dark wood, those in the middle of raw waxed steel. The orthogonal order of these display fittings allows the clothes to be placed informally, almost carelessly, encouraging the customers to linger and touch. Rearranging the seasonal exhibits is a simple and straightforward task in the minimal interior.

The collection of simple basic forms, of strong dark elements against plain white painted walls creates a dramatic interior of light and shade.

'…like our furniture, the all-important thing about our architecture is that it must be transformable. That's why we need a departure point. A point that contains centrifugal forces, an idea around which the whole project can pivot.'

Claudio Lazzarini

Above:
View through the space
The dynamic quality of the furniture creates an illusion of three-dimensional movement.

Facing page, above:
Interior display elements
Accessories are placed almost carelessly upon the sliding planes.

Facing page, below:
Three-dimensional drawing of the interior
Display units organise and accentuate the volume of the interior.

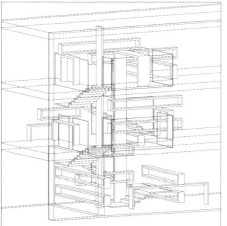

Transferability
The concept for a particular assembled interior can be transferred to anywhere in the world, because there is little relationship between the building and the new interior, it is really only a matter of how much of the design can be used at each location.

'Para-site is a site specific installation (which) takes up the theme of a filtered vision in the museum.
As parasiting is by nature site specific, a closer reading of the organism is unavoidable.'

Diller Scofidio + Renfro

Assembled: Focus study 3

Name:
'Para-site' exhibition

Location:
New York, USA

Date:
1989

Designer:
Diller Scofidio + Renfro

An assembled installation can inhabit apparently arbitrary places within an interior, without altering the building, or being altered by it. The radical design practice, Diller Scofidio + Renfro created such an installation at the Museum of Modern Art in New York. The exhibition questioned the premise upon which people visit a museum, was it to view the exhibits or was it to be seen within the confines of a museum?

The installation observed and recorded the visitors' reactions to the museum. Video cameras were positioned above the revolving entrance door of the museum, other CCTV cameras monitored the escalators, while cameras attached to convex security mirrors were placed within the sculpture court, all to capture images of the museum visitors. These images were then relayed to a series of monitors within the gallery spaces. Although the TV screens were fairly standard, the structure that supported them was an extended construction made of individual elements with exposed fixings and trailing wires.

The escalators, revolving doors, corridors and shop spaces are also the standard elements of shopping malls and convenience stores and, as such, they are the elements that inhabit the spaces of commerce and consumption. The live feeds from the elevators, escalators, thresholds and courtyard relayed images of the approaching visitors to the viewers in the gallery, thus blurring the distinction between the subject and the object; the viewer and the viewed.

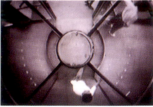

Top:
The installation
Standard television monitors contrast strongly with the bespoke structural supports.

Above:
Entrance surveillance
An unsuspecting museum visitor becomes the subject of the exhibition.

Above:
View through the gallery
The invasive quality of the
installation dominates
the white space of the gallery.

Right:
Diagram of the project
The installation is an assembled
collection of standard parts.

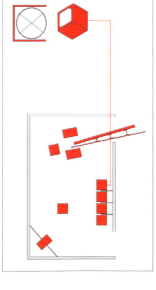

The interiors in this category utilise both the assembled and disguised approaches to organising interior space. The existing space is regarded as a neutral box that is lined and then inhabited by a series of elements.

Below:
The interior spaces
The yellow rubber lining of the private dining space has an intimate glow.

Below:
Passage between the forms
Brushed aluminium cladding appears to erupt from the grid of the floor.

Combined: Focus study 1

Name:
Restaurant Georges, Pompidou Centre

Location:
Paris, France

Date:
1997

Designer:
Jakob + Macfarlane

An autonomous design can be considered to be free standing with little or no connection to the site in which it is placed. Both the disguised and the assembled strategies have been used in this project.

Restaurant Georges occupies the sixth floor of the Pompidou Centre, the groundbreaking arts centre designed by Rogers and Piano in 1977. The new interior not only could not touch the listed HVAC fittings, but it also had to be incredibly lightweight to avoid any heavy loading on the thin slab floors. The design of the restaurant is based on a tacit acknowledgement of the dominating structural grid, yet the designers imploded the constraining frame and, through digital manipulation, created a design whereby a series of outrageously swollen globular forms house the various activities of the restaurant.

The new oversized brushed aluminium shapes burst out of the floor grid to become organic bulbous containers for different functions; the bar, private dining space, reception, kitchen and toilets. The interiors of these are coated with coloured rubber: yellow for dining, red for bar, grey for the kitchen and green for reception and toilets.

A floor of matching aluminium was laid over the existing floor and it is this skin that is distorted, thus creating a new interior that disregards the unrelenting intellectual logic of the original building, but explodes in colourful anarchy.

Autonomous interiors

Above:
View of the pods
Swollen globular pods contrast
with the orthogonal organisation
of the Pompidou Centre.

Left:
The dining space
The dining space is organised
according to the 800mm grid
of the rest of the building – even
the chairs are 800mm wide.

Assembled > Combined

'Whether it be concerned with the treatment of surfaces…
or the objects that make it up…aesthetics has an
increasing hold on objective reality.'

François Burkhardt

Combined: Focus study 2

Name:
Alexander McQueen Store

Location:
New York, USA

Date:
2002

Designer:
William Russell

1
Sudjic, D.
Domus Fashion Supplement.
Vol. no. 858 p.52

An autonomous interior has
the ability to entirely conceal the
existing shell or space and to
create a completely new interior
in which practically nothing
of the original space is evident.

The interior of this Alexander
McQueen shop has the qualities
of a single sculptured form:
the space feels as if it has been
hollowed out of a solid block
rather than constructed piece
by piece. The store is dominated
by the curves of one plane
meeting another. The blue/white
walls blend seamlessly into the
ceiling and pearlised terrazzo floor
and the walls curve horizontally
into each other. The room is
completely disguised. Huge
sculptural display cabinets hang
from the ceiling, reasserting the
ice, cold and frozen metaphor.

These giant icicles glow with
blue light and exhibit the clothes
and accessories, leaving brightly
lit empty space beneath them.
This image is accentuated by the
horizontal stripe of light placed
around the shop at door-head
height, which bestows an eerie
glow upon the interior. The
centre of the shop is dominated
by a smooth, sculptured structure
that arcs gracefully from floor to
ceiling and conceals the elegant
walnut-veneered fitting rooms.

The Alexander McQueen store
was conceived as a sort of '*Close
Encounters of the Third Kind
on Ice*'[1], futuristic film set. The
flagship store completely fills the
available space and the building
is just the receptacle to hold
and receive the new elements.

Right:
Diagram of the interior
The internal organisation of the
shop completely disguises the
shape of the original building.

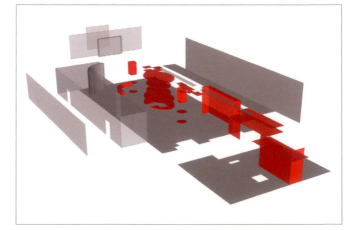

Above:
Display elements
Central units hover above the reflective surface of the floor.

Left:
View towards the front of the interior
The space appears to be carved from a solid piece of ice.

Assembled > Combined

Combined: Focus study 3

Name:
APOC for Issey Miyake

Location:
Paris, France

Date:
2000

Designer:
Bouroullec Brothers

Function can often be the generating factor for the design of an interior; it can be substantially more influential than the quality of the space itself. The objects that are to be used within the space will often influence the creation of an autonomous interior.

The new elements of an interior can be insubstantial, quite slight, thin and fairly lightweight, and yet so vivid that they dominate the space that they inhabit. This is the approach taken by Bouroullec Brothers when designing the APOC store for Issey Miyake. The interior of the shop is clad with lines of clean white and brightly coloured Corian (a solid mouldable plastic). Just three colourful horizontal lines form the space: they circumnavigate the room, attached to, but proud of the plain white painted walls. They define and give character to the otherwise anonymous shop. Bright folded units also from the same plastic material, then populate the interior. They stretch and extend into the shop, hovering graciously in the centre, to act as a cutting table, an ironing board, or simply to display the clothes.

The concept came directly from a process of producing continuous tubes of fabric developed by Miyake. A computer will programme an industrial knitting or weaving machine with the customer requirements, and this creates the clothing from a single unbroken thread. A truly industrial process, the thread goes in at one end and the finished piece of clothing emerges from the other. The customer is encouraged to participate in the design process, so the interior acts as a studio, factory and shop.

The new elements define the shape and character of the unspecific area – it is a process that can be adapted for practically any interior. The design was generated by the nature of the products on sale and the process used to construct them.

Above:
Diagram of the interior
Coloured lines organise and control the interior.

Top left:
Garment display
Garments are quite casually
displayed in the space.

Top centre:
View of the interior
The lines of corian disguise the
form of the original building.

Top right:
Colourful objects in the space
These organising elements
also display the clothes.

Above:
Fabric and clothing displays
Central display units slide
through the space.

Assembled > Combined

The strategy for organising space will inform the plan or layout of a building, but it is the elements within the space that actually give it personality: what it feels like, how it sounds, what it looks like. The elements are the individual components of the building, the separate details. They are an expression of the use and of the character of a building. It is these elements that distinguish or make different one place from another. The elements give character; they define the quality and provide the features of a building and it is the tactical deployment of them that gives the remodelled building or space its individual nature. The whole building can be understood through the reading of the details. For example, the design of a strategically placed element, such as a wall or a staircase can be very different depending upon the circumstance. Its position, the materials that it is constructed from, its individual purpose and the pursuit of the designer will all contribute to the design. It is the relationship between these individual and specific elements that will impart atmosphere, personality and disposition.

Name:
Vitra Fire Station

Location:
Weil am Rein, Germany

Date:
1994

Designer:
Zaha Hadid

Top to bottom:

Reactor Film Studio, USA,
by Pugh & Scarpa.

The Brasserie, USA,
by Diller Scofidio + Renfro

The British Museum, UK,
by Foster + Partners.

Object

An object or series of objects can provide focus to
a space, facilitate or encourage movement, supply
rhythm or balance and promote direction, both visual
and physical. They can be at the scale of an objet d'art
or piece of furniture, or they can possibly be much
larger constructions, such as pods or pavilions.

Plane

Planes are normally vertical or horizontal, mostly taking
the form of walls and floors or ceilings. They define
and organise in that they control the visual and physical
limits of a space. But they can be so much more than
a pure surface; walls can act as containers, they can
hide or disguise things, ceilings can create atmosphere
or indicate route and floors can give clarity and direction.

Sequence

Sequence is generally referred to as circulation;
it is usually either vertical or horizontal, and takes the
form of stairs, lifts, or paths or corridors. These areas
of circulation are often the only public spaces in
a building and as such, can serve to bind the disparate
activities together.

Elements for organising space

Top to bottom:

Chapel of Resurrection, Sweden,
by Sigurd Lewerentz.

Storefront for Art & Architecture, USA,
by Steven Holl and Vito Acconci.

Groninger Museum, the Netherlands,
by Philippe Starck.

Light

Light will reveal space and define form. Whether natural
or artificial, it can accentuate objects or spaces, suggest
direction and aid the understanding of a building. Light
is an essential element and the skilful articulation of it can
influence the experience of a building.

Threshold

Thresholds establish physical and visual relationships
between objects and places. They can indicate the
next part of the journey or become a reminder of things
already experienced. They can be highly decorated
and reveal the end of one encounter and the beginning
of the next, or they can be so modest that they do not
interfere with the experience of the journey at all.

Texture

The texture of an element describes the very materials
that it is made from. It is the stuff that is touched, felt
or handled. The specific choice of materials imparts
character; this surface establishes a direct relationship
between human contact and the building. It not only
has to provide ergonomic and environmental strength
when necessary, but also has to signal personality.

The deployment of an object can provide focus to a space. Whether the scale of the element is small or large its use enables movement, supplies rhythm or balance and facilitates function.

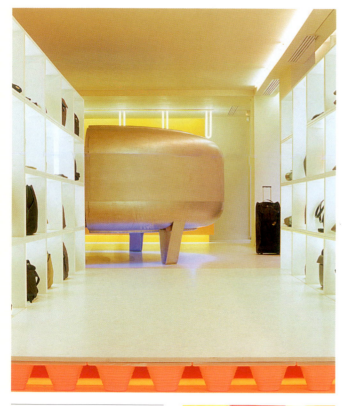

Above:
View towards the retail unit
The enigmatic circular display unit conceals the accessories.

Right:
Display wall
Handbags are strapped to the wall element with gigantic rubber bands.

Object: Focus study 1

Name:
Mandarina Duck Store

Location:
Paris, France

Date:
2001

Designer:
Droog Design

An object, when used at a particular scale, can be the primary organising element of a space. Instead of just facilitating the arrangement of space, it can control it. Within retail design, the idiosyncratic qualities of an object can communicate an identifiable message that is specifically related to the items for sale. The eccentric or peculiar characteristics of the designed objects can be imbued with the projected lifestyle that the products offer.

Droog created an interior based on a series of elements or cocoons for the flagship Mandarina Duck store in Paris. These objects: circle, tunnel, wall, curtain and enclosure, were then translated into elements for organising interior space and displaying the collection of bags, clothes and accessories.

Elements for organising space

Object: Focus study 2

Name:
Apartment

Location:
New York, USA

Date:
1975

Designer:
George Ranalli

A freestanding object can be designed to accommodate and contain a number of different functions. Separate activities can be collected together to form a tight single element. In a small domestic space, it can be economical to combine the seating, storage, eating, and sleeping activities together, to create one piece of furniture that can contain all of these needs.

In a tiny apartment in a warehouse in New York, George Ranalli has created such a piece of furniture. It consists of a dining space below a raised sleeping platform, which is accessed by a stair that contains bookshelves, with steps that are wide and deep enough to relax upon. The distinct object combines many of the functions necessary to create a suitable space for living.

Above:
Interior element
The free-standing piece
of multi-use furniture.

Top:
The meeting room
The shipping container
is remodelled to house the
meeting room.

Above:
The view from the street
The container acts as an
advert for the studio in the
shop window.

Object: Focus study 3

Name:
Reactor Film Studio

Location:
Los Angeles, USA

Date:
1996

Designer:
Pugh & Scarpa

A ready-made object can create
surprise and interest when it is
removed from its natural context
and placed within unfamiliar
surroundings. Despite the fact
that conceptual artists have been
using found objects for almost
a century, it is still a provocative
and challenging act for a designer
to relocate items that have
a specific use and context
into a different environment.

Pugh & Scarpa installed
a shipping container in the
'shop window' at the front of the
Reactor Film Studio. This unusual
element was adapted to contain
the meeting room; a small flight
of stairs was installed and a door,
windows and other opening
were cut into the container.
More importantly, it has become
a signal of the creative process
within the building.

Readymade
Marcel Duchamp developed the term 'readymade'
in 1915 to refer to found objects chosen by the artist
as art. Duchamp assembled the first readymade,
'Bicycle Wheel' in 1913, and in 1917, 'Fountain',
a urinal, which he signed with the pseudonym 'R. Mutt',
shocked the art world.

'Whether avant-garde or mainstream,
all designed objects, and chairs in
particular, can be understood as a channel
of communication between people.'
Charlotte & Peter Fiell

Object: Focus study 4

Name:
Magna Science Adventure Centre

Location:
Rotherham, UK

Date:
2001

Designer:
Wilkinson Eyre

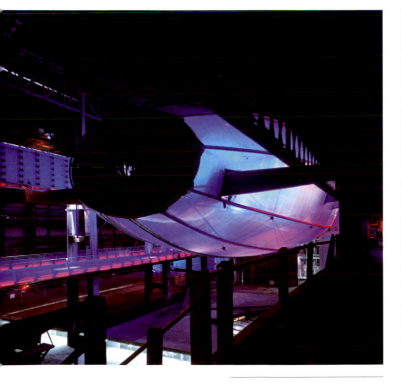

Scale is a very important
consideration when designing
interiors. If an object is too
small, it could potentially be
lost, too large and it could
be overpowering.

The Templeborough Steelworks
was once the largest smelting
plant in Europe and the architects
chose to use appropriately
huge elements to organise
the space in its remodelling.
The experience-based science
adventure museum was installed
within the massive shed and
the rusted decrepit shell of the
building was treated as the
backdrop for a series of four
new pavilions placed within
the space. The pavilions house
interactive exhibitions and
each is dedicated to a different
basic element: fire, water, earth
and air. The contrast between
the decrepit building and
the gleaming pods is dynamic
and extreme.

Above:
The new object
The internally illuminated
Air Pavilion hangs from the
original crane rail in the shed.

Whether a wall, floor or ceiling, a plane will define and organise space. It controls its visual and physical limits, directs movement, contains texture and manipulates light.

Above:
The shop interior
The undulating horizontal plane links the ground floor with the basement.

Plane: Focus study 1

Name:
Prada Store

Location:
New York, USA

Date:
2001

Designer:
Rem Koolhaas/OMA
(Office for Metropolitan Architecture)

A floor can control movement and circulation through a space. The Prada store in New York manipulates both the physical and visual connection between the front and rear of the shop. The store occupies the ground floor and basement of a very long and narrow nineteenth-century warehouse. The undulating floor exaggerates and amplifies the sheer length of the space, to produce what might be described, not as an interior, but as a landscape.

The blonde zebra wood surface swoops down from the entrance to unite the basement and ground-floor levels, it is a sinuous wave of floor that surfs through the long thin space from ground level into the basement and then back up to realign itself with the entrance at the rear of the shop.

Rem Koolhaas
In his highly influential book, *S,M,L,XL*, Rem Koolhaas articulated his theory of 'Bigness', the idea that the contextual architectural principles (composition, scale, proportion, detail) no longer apply when a building acquires 'Bigness'.

Plane: Focus study 2

Name:
The Brasserie

Location:
New York, USA

Date:
2000

Designer:
Diller Scofidio + Renfro

A plane need not be horizontal, vertical or flat. The focal point of The Brasserie restaurant is a huge timber surface that wraps around the dining area. It is constructed from a series of interconnected, overlapping sheets of veneered pearwood. The screen is changed and deformed depending upon the function; it is folded to become a bench seat at ground level and it floats vertically to contain the dining area before it is suspended horizontally from the ceiling. Structure and services are concealed behind the screen, thus giving the impression that it is both hovering and unconstrained.

Above:
The restaurant
The pearwood plane wraps around the dining area.

Left:
View across the dining space
The plane is constructed from overlapping sheets of veneered pearwood. This allows it to conceal lighting, to become seating and to define the dining space.

Plane: Focus study 3

Name:
Basilica

Location:
Vicenza, Italy

Date:
1549

Designer:
Andrea Palladio

Palladio's remodelling of the large, slightly uneven town hall was an ingenious solution to the problem of not only how to support the building, but also how to order and regulate it.

The existing building, which had partially collapsed, was wrapped with a new façade. This solution gives an impression of uniformity to an irregular building and site. Palladio's structure could not be called a building; it was a screen around the existing building that functioned as both a buttressing device and an elegantly decorated wall. The new construction was predetermined by the form of the original building, the position, the height of the two storeys and the width and number of bays. Classical architecture is ordered and balanced, and Palladio accommodated the existing irregularity by using Serlio's arch-lintel system. The façade was divided into bays, each opening was flanked by columns and it was the gap between the column and the edge of the bay that absorbed the inconsistencies. Thus the arches are all the same height and the building appears to be regular.

'The façade is…the most essential architectural element capable of communicating the function and significance of a building…It speaks of the cultural situation at the time that the building was built; it reveals criteria of order and ordering, and gives an account of the possibilities and ingenuity of ornamentation and decoration. A façade also tells us about the inhabitants of a building.'

Rob Krier

Above:
The view from the main square in Vicenza
The classical order of the new façade is clearly visible as it wraps around the old building.

Plane: Focus study 4

Name:
Santa Caterina Market

Location:
Barcelona, Spain

Date:
2006

Designer:
EMBT (Enric Miralles–Benedetta Tagliabue)

The Santa Caterina Market reconstruction was part of a much larger redevelopment of a rundown part of the Gothic Quarter of Barcelona. EMBT have gutted and then recovered the original building with an undulating roof of vivid colours. The architects retained the white painted masonry walls on three sides of the rectangular 1845 market structure, with many arched openings permeable to the surrounding streets. The new roof hovers above these retained walls, scarcely touching or even acknowledging them. It acts as an enormous blanket that controls the climate within the market while still allowing air movement through the building.

The undulating structure hangs from four steel arches supported by a steel and timber framework, the exposed services are clearly visible. The roof panels are constructed from laminated timber and the surface is finished in hexagonal ceramic tiles. It is this element that is so vibrant and dramatic, a pixelated representation of the market produce.

Top:
The old and the new
The new roof hovers above the walls of the original building.

Above:
Drawing of an aerial view
A drawing of the roof in context.

The sequence or circulation through a building or space can be vertical or horizontal and usually takes the form of stairs, lifts, corridors and paths.

Sequence: Focus study 1

Name:
Felix Nussbaum Museum

Location:
Osnabrück, Germany

Date:
1998

Designer:
Daniel Libeskind

The corridor is the backbone of interior circulation, the organisation of contemporary space would be impossible without it, and yet strangely, it is a relatively recent invention. It was first used in the seventeenth century as an expedient method of separating the servants from those that they served. The corridor can link spaces and rooms, it can provide a pause, it can even tell a story.

The architect Daniel Libeskind used this seemingly innocuous element as a narrative device to symbolise the traumatic journey of the persecuted Jewish painter, Felix Nussbaum, in a gallery dedicated to him. The gallery, which is an extension of the old Osnabrück Museum, consists of a series of rooms, each of which is orientated toward one of the various destinations that became a place of refuge for the artist. The galleries contain the paintings that he managed to produce when hidden in the attics or spare rooms of sympathisers, while the interior circulation is a metaphor for this journey. At the end of the final corridor is a symbol of the termination of the painter's flight: a stark metal door with a cross on it.

Above:
Aerial view of the museum
The dramatic juxtaposition of the extension with the original building.

Left:
The corridor
The emotional journey of Nussbaum's life is evocatively portrayed in the central corridor.

Above:
The courtyard interior
The substantial Spanish limestone staircase.

Name:
Great Court, British Museum

Location:
London, UK

Date:
2000

Designer:
Foster + Partners

The staircase provides vertical circulation between floor levels. It can be an uninspiring arrangement, suitable only as an emergency exit or it can be an elaborate sculptural form that creates a focal point for the interior.

The British Museum, constructed between 1823 and 1859 by Sir Robert Smirke, is one of London's main tourist attractions. The clearing, refurbishment and covering of the courtyard by Foster + Partners created a generous circulation and meeting area within the heart of the building. The most dominant feature of the remodelling is the new complex glazed roof that covers this inside/outside space. However, the two elliptical staircases that surround the great circular reading room are a much more sensitive interpretation of the old building. They not only provide access to the restaurant and temporary gallery on the first floor but they also allow the visitor to observe the activities in the courtyard. They appear as strong and distinguished elements and are constructed from the same Spanish limestone as the rest of the building. They provide a thoughtful and respectful addition to the space.

Right:
The ascent
The ramps provide a dignified and leisurely route to the upper galleries.

Below:
The ramp bathed in light
The sequence of ramps is bathed in natural light.

Name:
Museum of Arts and Crafts

Location:
Frankfurt, Germany

Date:
1985

Designer:
Richard Meier

The ramp offers a useful alternative to stairs as a method of moving vertically through a building. It encourages all of the building's users to elegantly glide through a space on a gently inclined plane. The primary disadvantage of the ramp is that it requires large swathes of interior space in order to make it accessible, that is, to comply with building regulations, particularly the Disability Discrimination Act (1995).

The Museum of Arts and Crafts in Frankfurt is a series of gleaming white modernist buildings, collected around the 200-year-old Villa Metzler. The ramp is an axial element that traverses and divides the buildings and is slightly out of alignment with the original house, thus accentuating the differences between the old and new. It protrudes slightly from the building and solemnly rises through the new spaces; it is this sense of movement that is used to link the various levels of the building.

Right:
View to the top floor
The escalator takes the visitor from the dark depths of the foyer to the bright upper floor.

Below:
The middle gallery
The escalator travels directly to the top floor, allowing visitors to descend via the stairs at their own pace.

Sequence: Focus study 4

Name:
National Portrait Gallery

Location:
London, UK

Date:
2000

Designer:
Dixon Jones

Escalators are synonymous with shopping centres, airports, train stations and department stores; they link different floor levels efficiently and move large numbers of people with minimum fuss. It is therefore a seemingly bizarre move for the notoriously sensitive architects Dixon Jones to use the longest escalator outside of the London Underground to traverse the triple-height foyer space of the National Portrait Gallery. And yet it does not appear to be out of place within the elegant white space in which it works. The visitor is encouraged to rise elegantly and conveniently through the new foyer into the light of the top floor of the gallery, and from there, they can descend through chronologically-arranged galleries at their own pace.

Disability Discrimination Act (1995)
The Disability Discrimination Act (1995) is an Act of UK law designed to end discrimination against disabled people. Part M of the Building Regulations 2004 is concerned with the access and use of buildings. It has a particular emphasis on the use of ramps to allow full access to all parts of a building.

Whether natural or artificial, light accentuates objects or spaces, suggests movement and circulation and aids the understanding of the interior of a building.

Light: Focus study 1

Name:
D.E. Shaw Office and
Trading Area

Location:
New York, USA

Date:
1992

Designer:
Steven Holl

Natural and artificial light can be combined to create an indefinite or uncertain atmosphere. The entrance area of the D.E. Shaw & Co. offices, on the top floor of a forty-storey tower block in New York, is a perfect white double-storey cube. Into the walls of this are carved alcoves and niches. There is an ambiguity to these recesses: some lead to further rooms within the office, some are windows, while others are just there for effect, leading nowhere. They are all coloured and lit from within, either naturally or artificially, depending upon the position. The illuminated colour is reflected in and around the notched spaces, thus projecting the colour towards the room and making very apparent that there are spaces beyond the entrance area. The uncertainty about the function of the alcoves creates a mysterious and enigmatic interior.

Above:
The reception
The illuminated niches provide light for the double height reception space.

Light: Focus study 2

Name:
Dulwich Picture Gallery

Location:
London, UK

Date:
1812

Designer:
Sir John Soane

Natural light can be manipulated to create rooms of great emotion and feeling. Light and shade together can be used to generate a narrative or sequence of differing atmospheres or spaces. Dulwich Picture Gallery is a very fine example of an interior that makes use of controlled light and movement through a series of rooms.

Francis Bourgeois bequeathed his fine collection of paintings as well as sufficient funds to build a gallery for them, to Dulwich College on two conditions; the first was that Sir John Soane was to be the architect and the second was that the gallery should contain his own mausoleum.

The plan form of the building suggests an antique catacomb, a progression of quite bright top-lit galleries. At the centre, is a dark side chamber that leads to the mausoleum; a serene reverential space that is bathed in amber-coloured natural light, from the yellow glass in the rooftop lantern.

Top:
The galleries
A progression of bright top-lit galleries.

Left:
The mausoleum
The mausoleum is quite dark in comparison to the galleries.

Sequence > Light > Threshold

Above and left:
Sequence of views
of the light installation
The subtle blue space
appears to recede into infinity.

'Sky Spaces'

James Turrell has created a series of works called
'Sky Spaces', which encourages the viewer to
become intensely conscious of the changing quality
of the sky. Each installation is a single room that is
entered through a tunnel. The light level in the space
is kept at a constant intensity. The room has no roof;
it is open to the sky. The viewer looks through this
framed gap into the upper atmosphere. The experience
is especially atmospheric at dawn or dusk, when
the changing sky is particularly noticeable.

Light: Focus study 3

Name:
'Light Installations'

Location:
Underground gallery, Yorkshire
Sculpture Park, UK

Date:
2006–07

Designer:
James Turrell

James Turrell works with both
natural and artificial light. In this
project at the Yorkshire Sculpture
Park, he bathes one end of the
underground gallery with blue
light, with the effect of blurring
the boundaries of the room. The
periphery of the gallery becomes
indistinct, it becomes difficult
to judge the depth of the
space – is it a view of nothing
or of infinity?

Turrell regards light as
a three-dimensional material
to be manipulated, controlled
and formed, or deformed.
He meticulously constructs his
installations by building screens
that control the size and shape
of the space. These are lit
with steady and unvarying
light – fittings that do not
become dim at the ends, thus
forming a constant and
continuous presence. The
level of light within the
installation is very low; the
room is murky, almost dark.
Turrell manipulates our
perception of what is there
and what is not.

'Architecture is the masterly, correct and magnificent play of masses brought together in light.'

Le Corbusier

Light: Focus study 4

Name:
Chapel of Resurrection,
Woodland Cemetery

Location:
Stockholm, Sweden

Date:
1925

Designer:
Sigurd Lewerentz

The Chapel of Resurrection is a simple, austere building with a detached classical open portico on the north façade and a wide tri-part window on the south. The entrance is at right angles to the axis of the building, and so the procession enters into the shadows of the nave before turning to face the altar. The interior is lit by just the one large off-centre, south-facing window, which floods the altar with brilliant light. The journey is one from the daylight of the cemetery, through the darkness of the portico and the shadows of the nave to the radiant brightness of the altar.

Above:
The chapel
The south light dramatically illuminates the altar.

The threshold marks the distinction between spaces and objects. It can indicate the next part of the journey or become a reminder of things already experienced.

Threshold: Focus study 1

Name:
Storefront for Art
& Architecture

Location:
New York, USA

Date:
1993

Designer:
Steven Holl and Vito Acconci

The openings in a façade of a building can be described as the threshold between the inside and the outside. The façade of a building is generally solid; masonry, timber, glass, and the openings are usually the doors and windows.

The Storefront for Art & Architecture has an adaptable façade, the solidity of the wall is punctured by a collection of cuts and openings. These are a series of orthogonal cut-out panels set into a solid screen wall. The panels are set on pivots that allow them to swing open, and depending upon the time, weather and the current show, they can be arranged in different compositions. This, in effect, eliminates the straightforward barrier between inside and outside, the gallery and the street. This is especially enchanting at night when the interior light explodes from the gallery inviting viewers into this little slice of inside-out New York space.

Top:
The façade of the gallery
The panels on the façade pivot open in order to diffuse the distinction between inside and out.

Above:
Detail of one of the panels
The open panels create a dramatic pattern of light and shade.

Elements for organising space

Threshold: Focus study 2

Name:
Comme des Garçons Store

Location:
New York, USA

Date:
1998

Designer:
Future Systems

The threshold is generally regarded as the point of transition from one space to another, that is, the point at which a new experience begins.

The Comme des Garçons store is situated in a particularly tough waterside area of New York. The interior of the shop is stark, bright and white and contrasts strongly with the nineteenth-century brick façade and the retained old signage and external industrial fire escapes. The entrance marks the transition between the grime, graffiti and general debris surrounding the shop and the cool clean interior. This change is acknowledged with an asymmetric tubular entrance structure made entirely from aluminium. It is both raw and refined, clean yet unfinished. The slightly swollen floor of the tube transports the shopper over the threshold; the edgy street attitude slips away and is lost in the white space of the interior.

Above:
View into the entrance tunnel
The contrast between the graffitied exterior and the shiny new threshold.

Right:
Concept sketch
A concept sketch shows the intended dramatic transition between inside and out.

Threshold: Focus study 3

Name:
National Gallery Extension

Location:
London, UK

Date:
1991

Designer:
Venturi, Scott Brown
and Associates

A route through a gallery is often more than a chronological journey through the history of art. The works of art themselves can be exhibited or displayed in a manner that accentuates both the work of art and the building. A relationship between the two can be developed.

The Sainsbury Wing, an extension to the National Gallery, exploits the axis that runs across and links the two buildings. The long route was continued from the courtyard of the original building into the extension, through a sequence of arches or individual thresholds. The perspective has been manipulated by diminishing the dimension of the arches, thus the journey is exaggerated and the focal point made more clear. At the end of the sequence is a work by Cima da Conegliano, *The Incredulity of Saint Thomas* (about 1502–04) that seems to prolong the development of the arches.

Above:
The framed view through the space
The painting is part of the sequence.

Left:
The painting framed by the arch
The visual journey continues into and through the threshold.

'The experience of entering a building influences the way you feel inside the building. If the transition is too abrupt there is no feeling of arrival, and the inside of the building fails to be an inner sanctum.'

Christopher Alexander

Threshold: Focus study 4

Name:
Picasso Museum

Location:
Paris, France

Date:
1986

Designer:
Roland Simounet

Thresholds can provide visual links as well as physical. They can offer glimpses of places previously visited, those still to be seen as well as supplying views of the surrounding context. They make important connections inside and outside the building.

Roland Simounet has created an intricate circulation route within the old townhouse in Paris. The existing doorways are used as framing devices for the views through the space, thus allowing the visitor glimpses of what is ahead, what has already been seen and of the outside. There is a view of the final gallery from the reception area and halfway through the exhibition the entrance courtyard is suddenly revealed from the first floor. The existing thresholds have been embellished and become frames for this series of views or scenes.

Above:
The gallery interior
The sequence of the gallery spaces is animated by both natural and artificial light.

The specific choice of materials imparts character upon a space and establishes a direct relationship between the people who occupy the space and the building itself.

Name:
Groninger Museum

Location:
Groningen, the Netherlands

Date:
1994

Designer:
Philippe Starck

The Groninger Museum is a collection of distinct buildings designed by different architects to house the four separate collections held by the museum. Alessandro Mendini was responsible for overseeing the whole project and Philippe Starck designed the pavilion for the applied art collection. The building is a huge circular steel drum positioned upon an apparently floating brick plinth, it has no windows and the interior is completely controlled by artificial light.

The gallery contains a series of tough, highly engineered glass and steel cases that hold beautiful, delicate porcelain teapots, cutlery and other objects. A diaphanous curtain surrounds these displays; it hangs from the ceiling and curves around the hard edges of each case, creating a tranquil, almost ethereal atmosphere. The visitor becomes a shadow through the translucent screens as they move through the space.

Above:
View into the display space
The sinuous curtain controls movement through the space.

Right:
The curtains
The hard-edged cases contrast with the soft fabric of the curtain.

Philippe Starck
The French designer, Philippe Starck (b.1949) is considered to be one of the most influential and creative designers of the late twentieth and early twenty-first century. His distinct creations range in scale from a toothbrush holder to large buildings.

Above:
The shop interior
The limited palette of materials creates an atmospheric interior.

Texture: Focus study 2

Name:
Johan Menswear shop
Location:
Graz, Austria
Date:
1992
Designer:
Claudio Silvestrin

A designer or architect can choose to work with a very limited palette of materials, which will effectively accentuate the qualities and characteristics of each and emphasise the contrast between them. This restrained style of using texture and surfaces is often referred to as minimalism. Identity can be communicated through this restrained and focused approach.

Claudio Silvestrin uses just three materials to organise and decorate the interior of this retail space. This spare and minimal quality is achieved using putty-coloured polished plaster for the walls, shelves, ceiling and cylindrical changing rooms. The floor is of polished concrete and the long central display plinth that slides through the vaulted space is of limed oak.

The design of the space is uncompromising and exact, everything is worked out to a demanding level and the workmanship is exact and precise, even down to the meticulous two-millimetre shadow gap between the floor and the walls.

'A coarse rough concrete finish has a quite different quality to that of polished marble and different again to studded rubber or fun fur, even though they can all quite viably be placed in an identical position.'

Brooker & Stone

Texture: Focus study 3

Name:
Castelvecchio Museum

Location:
Verona, Italy

Date:
1964

Designer:
Carlo Scarpa

Texture is an important element for organising space and is generally used in one of two ways: 'applied' or 'found'. 'Applied' is the method of cladding or lining a space with a specific material, whereas 'found' makes use of existing textures, which are retained and incorporated into the new design.

A common feature of Scarpa's work was to leave a small gap between new and existing materials, thus creating clarity and emphasising both, and an example of this can be seen at the Castelvecchio Museum. The new stone floors of the galleries stop short of the existing walls. The vertical pink Prun stone slabs, which are placed at the threshold of each room and accentuate the junction between new and old, are slightly proud and the sculptures are separated from the floor and placed upon floating plinths.

Above:
Sculpture display
The polished pigmented plaster of the display screen highlights the delicate qualities of the objects.

Texture: Focus study 4

Name:
Royal Court Theatre

Location:
London, UK

Date:
1999

Designer:
Haworth Tompkins

When remodelling an existing building, the designer can take the very site-specific approach of uncovering the accretions and layers of the place and incorporating these into the redesign. This strategy of using 'found' texture is often connected to the history of the building and is an approach that allows the designer to expose the scratches and indentations of the building's evolution.

Haworth Tompkins wanted to emphasise the spirit of the theatre company by providing an edgy unusual space. This involved exposing the archaeology of layers of the floors and walls and contrasting these with new elements. The reception, bar and theatre are strong autonomous elements that stand out against their dilapidated surroundings.

Above:
The theatre foyer
The shiny new reception contrasts with the dilapidated building.

Many of the methods of organising and assembling interior space have been presented and a number of specialist terms introduced. While it is impossible to be exhaustive, a good number of these have been collected together in the following glossary to provide an easy reference section.

Adaptation The process of transforming an existing building to accommodate new uses. This is also referred to as remodelling, adaptive reuse and interior architecture.

Analysis The act of exploring and studying an existing building. This can be done in a variety of ways in order to extract the meaningful qualities of the building to prompt or stimulate the process of transforming the space.

Applied texture Added material such as metal, fabric, plastic or timber that can be applied to an existing surface in order to create or shape the new visual and atmospheric identity of an interior.

Arch A structural device that allows openings to be formed in a wall or façade. It is a curved structure, capable of spanning a space while supporting the significant weight of the wall above.

Axis An imaginary line that usually runs through the centre of a space or building, it is used as a planning device and is related to symmetry. Axial planning can be used to arrange an interior in straight lines or in a way that prioritises certain qualities such as a view through the space or emphasises hierarchy.

Baroque The style of the seventeenth century that fostered an exuberant period in all of the arts. In architecture the Baroque style was characterised by a florid, theatrical style, distinguished by elaborating Renaissance style elements in a sculptural and exaggerated fashion.

Beam A core component of a basic structural frame. It is a horizontal bar, usually made from masonry, steel, or timber that is supported at either end.

Circulation The methods of movement within a building. It is often arranged as a series of horizontal routes through a building via walkways, corridors and bridges, or vertically via stairs, ramps, lifts and escalators.

Cladding The application of a layer of material that will cover the structure of a building or element. On the outside of a building this may have to consider weathering and climate control. In an interior, cladding is more important in terms of performance, look and identity. The relationship between cladding and structure and its visual appearance is a complex issue that dominates architectural and design history. See Loos's Ornament and Crime, 1908.

Classical Classical architecture derives its principles from Greek and Roman art and architecture. The main orders of classical architecture are Tuscan, Doric, Ionic, Corinthian and Composite. In its revived style known as neo-classicism.

Column The column, along with the beam, forms the basic component of the structural system. It is the vertical element of the frame and is usually made from masonry, steel or timber.

Composition The plan or arrangement of elements in a visual design. In interior planning it relates to the organisation of the components of space. In elevations or sections composition can relate to the deployment of rooms and interior elements in the building.

Conservation The art of conserving existing structures in their present form or returning them back to their original state.

Context The conditions surrounding the building to be reused. These conditions may be in close proximity or far away and have a variety of impacts upon the new interior.

Design process The method by which a new design is created and realised.

Detail The finalising of a space and the application of materials and surfaces to an interior scheme is known as detailing. This often involves joinery, the application of materials and sometimes prototyping through mock-ups and samples.

Element Within an interior, a specific object such as a piece of furniture or a room is described as an 'element' within the space.

Elevation An elevation is a drawing usually of an outside wall or façade of a building. It is a two-dimensional representation of a wall showing the position of windows, doors and any other details of the building exterior.

Environment Environment refers to the context of a building and its interior and also refers to climatic issues with the design scheme or existing building.

Façade Quite simply the exterior front plane of a building.

Form follows form The notion that the design of an interior space is influenced by the qualities of the space in which it is being built.

Form follows function Form Follows Function is the modernist declaration that new buildings and interior spaces are determined by the functions that take place inside of them.

Found texture When working with existing buildings, surfaces within the space can be retained and used to provide meaningful connections to the original site.

Fractal A geometric shape that can be subdivided into parts, all of which are a reduced-size copy of the whole. Fractal relates to unusual geometries that may be used to generate complex and unusual forms for building design; this may need the help of sophisticated computer software.

Free Plan A system of design that uses a framed structure, and thus removes the need for load-bearing walls, creating a freedom and flexibility to the space.

Function The use of a space, either new or old, will often be referred to as the function of the space. Quite often function will also be referred to as 'the programme' of the interior or the accommodation brief for the new design.

Geometry Geometry is the field of studying the spatial relationships between things and is closely related to mathematics. In architecture and design, it relates to the systematic organisation of building spaces and elements.

Gothic revival The Gothic revival was an architectural movement that originated in England in the nineteenth century and sought to revive the medieval or pointed style in response to the prevailing neo-classical style of the time.

Hierarchy When organising and planning space, the word hierarchy is sometimes used to distinguish primary and secondary elements within a design. It may also be used to classify major and minor functions within a space.

H.V.A.C. Acronym for heating ventilation and air conditioning.

Interior architecture Interior architecture is the practice of remodelling existing buildings. As well as the robust reworking of a building interior architecture often deals with complex structural, environmental and servicing problems. It is sometimes referred to as adaptation, adaptive reuse or remodelling.

Interior decoration Interior decoration is the art of decorating inside spaces and rooms to impart a particular character and atmosphere to the room. It is often concerned with such issues as surface pattern, ornament, furniture, soft furnishings and lighting.

Interior design Interior design is an interdisciplinary practice that is concerned with the creation of a range of interior environments that articulate identity and atmosphere, through the manipulation of spatial volume, the placement of specific objects and furniture and the treatment of surfaces.

Listed building When a building, interior, monument or bridge is considered to be of historic importance or of cultural significance and therefore in need of protection from demolition or any insensitive changes, it is placed upon a protected building list. The listing usually takes the form of a grading of importance from one through to three.

Load bearing Load bearing is a term that refers to the structural system employed to construct the building. It refers to a structure that is usually masonry and built up brick by brick from the ground.

Monocoque A construction technique that uses the external skin of the object for structural support. The internal structure and the skin are unified as a single element. This is a method of construction most prevalent in aircraft and automotive design, but is beginning to be used as an architectural construction technique.

Narrative Narrative is a story or a text that describes a sequence of characters and events. In architecture and design, narrative is used to describe the stories or the sequence of events that the designer may wish to convey: whether an existing building, an exhibition design, or the concept or brand identity of a space.

Object A purposefully placed object is loaded with meaning; whether it is a small piece of furniture, a large sculpture or a number of pieces clustered together, it establishes a physical and cultural relationship with its environment.

Organisation Organisation can be described as the planning or arrangement of a space; that is the objects, rooms and elements.

Ornament An ornament is a decorative detail than can be used to embellish parts of a building or an interior. It is often superfluous and it became a highly debated element of design in the twentieth century.

Plane The façade, wall, ceiling and floor are regarded as the essential 'planes' of the interior and a building.

Plan Libre See Free Plan.

Planning The organisation of an interior by arranging the rooms, spaces and structure in a two-dimensional drawing.

Playstation organisation An organisational technique where a collection of events or objects are arranged in series, each is a complete entity and has to be fully appreciated before the viewer or competitor can move on. Similar to the organisational technique used in computer games.

Portico A roofed space, often open or partly enclosed that forms the entrance to a building. It developed in early Greek architecture, and is often supported by columns and can be a grand device on the façade of a building.

Promenade One of Le Corbusier's five points of architecture, it is the modernist concept of continual movement through a building. This journey is also referred to as architectural promenade.

Raumplan The Viennese architect Adolf Loos devised the Raumplan (Space Plan), it is best exemplified in the designs for the Müller and Moller houses in Prague and Vienna. The houses consist of a series of compact, enclosed and intimately connected rooms. Movement between them often organised in a complex manner.

Readymade The development of art from utilitarian everyday found objects not normally considered as art in their on right. The term readymade was coined by the artist, Marcel Duchamp, who created a series of objet d'art from such off-the-peg items as a bicycle wheel, a bottle rack and a urinal.

Renovation Renovation is the process of renewing and updating a building. The function will remain the same and the structure is generally untouched, but the manner in which the building is used will be brought up to date. It is usually the services that require attention, especially the heating and sanitary systems.

Remodelling The process of wholeheartedly altering a building. The function is the most obvious change, but other alterations may be made to the building such as its structure, circulations routes and its orientation. Additions may be constructed while other areas may be demolished.

Restoration The process of returning the condition of the building to its original state, often involving materials and techniques of the original period.

Reuse The transformation of an existing building, 'reuse' suggests that the elements and parts of both new and old building are reworked in order to create a new space. See also adaptation, remodelling and interior architecture.

Section At any point on the plan of a building, the designer may describe a line through the drawing and visualise a vertical cut through the spaces. This is called a section, it will explain the volumes of the spaces and indicate the position of the walls, the floors, the roof and other structural elements.

Sequence The order of interior spaces that the designer intends the visitor to experience in their journey through the space.

Site-specific The site is the specific location or context of a building or space. Site-specific is a phrase used to describe the influences that are derived directly from the particular conditions found on site.

Spolia Spolia describes the act of reusing building elements and applying them to new or later monuments. It derives from the phrase 'the spoils of war' where the victors in battle would take trophies from their foes.

Sustainability In architecture and design, the sensible use of natural resources in the construction and design industry, materials used in a way that does not deplete them in an unnecessary or wasteful way. Sustainability also refers to the sourcing and use of methods of construction and certain materials that do not contribute to climate change through the exhaustion of natural resources or their transport across the world.

Structure A shelter, or an enclosure that distinguishes inside and outside space. Structure is one of the basic elements of the construction of space and usually takes the form of materials assembled in such a way as to withstand the pressures put upon them.

Threshold The threshold is the point of transition between two spaces, whether this is inside and outside or two interior spaces.

Truss A truss is a number of beams and/or rafters tied together to form a bridging element.

Weather boarding A cladding method that uses timber to cover a building by successively overlapping each member, thus allowing the rain to run off and make a water-tight seal.

Graeme Brooker would like to thank Howard Cooper, Shelley McNulty and Michael Coates (Interior Design team at Manchester Metropolitan University) for their support and tea-making offers and Claire Brooker for her stoicism.

Sally Stone would like to thank Reuben, Ivan and Agnes for their resilience and Dominic Roberts for his fortitude.

Both Graeme Brooker and Sally Stone would like to thank Aaron Losada for the production of the excellent drawings, Holger Haas for the 'black series' photographs of the interior of the Loos Bar, MIRIAD (Manchester Institute of Research in Art and Design) for their financial assistance; all of the designers and photographers who have lent their work for publication, Ro Spankie and Garry Layden and finally, AVA publishing, especially Leafy Robinson, for all their help and support throughout the project.

Images

All diagrams by Aaron Losada and images © Graeme Brooker and Sally Stone, except for:

Cover photograph: Emma Cross, courtesy of Multiplicity

006: photograph by Christian Richters, courtesy of EEA

016+017: drawings by Ben Kelly Design

018+019: photograph and drawing by Francis Roberts Architects

022: photograph by Mohsen Mostafavai

025: photograph (top) by John Kurtich

038+039: photographs by Jonathan Keenan, courtesy of OMI Architects

042: drawing by O.M. Ungers

046+047: photographs by Brian Yeats, courtesy of Malcom Fraser Architects

050+051: photographs by Christian Richters, courtesy of EEA Architects

056: photograph by Nils Becker

059: drawing by Diller + Scofidio

060: main photograph by Roland Dafis/arcaid.co.uk; photographs below courtesy of S+ARCKNetwork

061: photograph courtesy of S+ARCKNetwork

062: drawing courtesy of Fielden Clegg Bradley Architects

063: photographs by Simon Doling, courtesy of Fielden Clegg Bradley Architects

064: photographs by Paul Ring

066+067: photographs by Paolo Pellion and Guido Fino, courtesy of Andrea Bruno Architects

097: diagrams by MVRDV

108+109: photographs and diagram courtesy of OMI Architects

116+117: photographs by Emma Cross, courtesy of Multiplicity

118+119: photograph by Chris Gascoigne, courtesy of View Pictures Ltd

120: diagrams courtesy of propeller z

126: diagrams (left and right, top) courtesy of 6a Architects; diagram (right, bottom) by Aaron Losada

127: photographs by David Grandorge, courtesy of 6a Architects

132: photograph by Farshid Assassi

133: photograph by Farshid Assassi; diagrams courtesy of Randy Brown Architects

134+135: photograph by Matteo Piazza; diagram courtesy of Lazzarini Pickering Studio

136+137: photographs courtesy of Diller + Scofidio

141: photographs by Frank Oudeman

142: diagram courtesy of Ronan and Erwan Bouroullec

143: photographs by Morgan Le Gall, courtesy of Ronan and Erwan Bouroullec

146: photograph (top) courtesy of Pugh & Scarpa

148: photographs by Wouter vandenBrink, courtesy of PAR31

149: photograph courtesy of George Ranalli

150: photographs courtesy of Pugh & Scarpa

151: photograph by Edmund Sumner, courtesy of View Pictures Ltd

155: drawing courtesy of EMBT Architects

156: photograph (top) by Bitter Bredt Fotographie

160: photograph by Paul Warchol

165: drawing courtesy of Future Systems

Pull quotes

017: Massey, A. 1990. *Interior Design of the 20th Century*. London: Thames & Hudson

019: Codman, O. Wharton, E. 1898. *The Decoration of Houses*. London: B.T. Batsford

028: Moore, R. 1992. *Sackler Galleries, Royal Academy*. London: Blueprint Extra 04

031: Cook, P. 1995. *Primer*. London: Academy Editions

037: Gregotti, V. 1996. *Inside Architecture*. Cambridge, MA: MIT Press

039: Cullen, G. 1996. *The Concise Townscape*. Oxford: The Architectural Press

041: Krier, R. 1983. *Elements of Architecture*. London: Architectural Design, Profile 49

042: Porter, T. 1997. *The Architect's Eye*. London: E&FN Spon

057: Vesely, D. 2004. *Architecture in the Age of Divided Representation*. Cambridge, MA: MIT Press

060: Turrell, J. 1987. *Mapping Spaces: A topological survey of the work of James Turrell*. New York: Peter Blum Editions

063: The Energy Research Group (Owen Lewis, J. (ed)). 1999. *A Green Vitruvius: Principles and Practice of Sustainable Architectural Design*. London: James & James (Science Publishers)

065: Blazwick, I. Wilson, S. 2000. *Tate Modern: The Handbook*. London: Tate Publishing

067: Schumacher, T. 1996. Contextualism: Urban Ideals and Deformations. In: Nesbitt, K. (ed). *Theorizing a New Agenda for Architecture Theory*. New Jersey: Princeton Architectural Press

071: Montaner, J.M. 1990. Basic Formal Concepts in Miralles' and Pinōs' Work. In: Buchanan, P., Kogod, K., Montaner, J.M. *The Architecture of Enric Miralles and Carme Pinōs*. Santa Fe: Lumen Books/SITES Books

074: Frampton, K. 1980. *Modern Architecture: A Critical History*. London: Thames & Hudson

075: Hebly, A. in Risselada, M. (ed.). 1989. *Raumplan Versus Plan Libre*. New York: Rizzoli

077: Andrea Palladio, quoted in Marton, P., Pape, T., Wundram, M. 2004. *Palladio: The Complete Buildings*. Köln: Taschen

078: Cohen, M. 2002. p.53. *Domus* 853

081: Ranalli, G. 1984. The Coherence of a Quest. In: Dal Co, F. Mazzariol, G. 1984. *Carlo Scarpa: The Complete Works*. Milan: Electa Editrice/Rizzoli

083: Weston, R. 2002. *Modernism*. London: Phaidon

096: Lootsma, B. 2000. *SuperDutch: New Architecture in the Netherlands*. New Jersey: Princeton Architectural Press

099: Krier, R. 1988. *Architectural Composition*. London: Academy Editions

091: Koolhaas, R. 1998. *OMA/Rem Koolhaas 1987–1998*. Madrid: El Croquis

093: Van Doesburg, T. 1924. 'Tot een beeldende architectuur'. *De Stijl*. 1 (6/7) p.80 In: Padovan, R. 2002. *Towards Universality: Le Corbusier, Mies and De Stijl*. London: Routledge

095: Hollein, H. 1985. Excerpt from his acceptance speech for the Pritzker Architecture Prize [online]. [Accessed 15 June 2007] www.pritzkerprize.com/full_new_site/hollein_acceptance.htm

097: Lootsma, B. 2000. *SuperDutch: New Architecture in the Netherlands*. New Jersey: Princeton Architectural Press

099: Pallasmaa, J. 2005 *Encounters. Architectural Essays*. Helsinki: Rakennustieto

106: Holl, S. 1989. *Anchoring: Selected Projects 1975–1988*. New Jersey: Princeton Architectural Press

111: Robert, P. 1989. *Adaptations: New uses for old buildings*. New Jersey: Princeton Architectural Press

118: Johan Jessen and Jochem Schneider, quoted in Schittich, C. (ed.) 2003. *Building in Existing Fabric*. Berlin: Birkhäuser Edition Detail

134: Lazzarini, C. 1998. *Frame Magazine*. July/August 1998

136: Diller, E. Scofidio, R. 1994. *Flesh: Architectural Probes*. London: Triangle Architectural Publishing

140: Burkhardt, F. 1997. *Domus Dossier*. Issue 5

151: Fiell, C. Fiell, P. 1997. *1000 Chairs*. Köln: Taschen

154: Krier, R. 1983. *Elements of Architecture*. London: Architectural Design, Profile 49

163: Le Corbusier, É. J. 1923. *Towards a New Architecture*. Paris

167: Alexander, C. 1977. *A Pattern Language*. Oxford: Oxford University Press

170: Brooker, G. Stone, S. 2004. *Re-Readings: Interior architecture and the design principles of remodelling existing buildings*. London: RIBA Publishing